MUSICOLOGICAL STUDIES AND DOCUMENTS

Armen Carapetyan, Ph. D
General Editor

SEBALD HEYDEN

DE ARTE CANENDI

AMERICAN INSTITUTE OF MUSICOLOGY

MUSICOLOGICAL STUDIES AND DOCUMENTS

26

SEBALD HEYDEN

DE ARTE CANENDI

Translation and Transcription

by

CLEMENT A. MILLER

AMERICAN INSTITUTE OF MUSICOLOGY

1972

TO

ARMEN CARAPETYAN

True friend of *ars musica*

CONTENTS

INTRODUCTION

The present edition of *De Arte Canendi* is based on the edition published by Petreius in Nürnberg in 1540.[1] Heyden considered *De Arte Canendi* to be the third edition, the first being *Musicae Στοιχείωσις* of 1532 and the second *Musicae, id est artis canendi libri duo* of 1537. Each edition is an enlargement of the preceding one, extending from 26 folios in *Musicae* of 1532 to 115 pages in *Musicae* of 1537 and finally to 163 pages in *De Arte Canendi* of 1540.

The original edition of *De Arte Canendi* begins with twelve unnumbered pages (f.A 1-6) devoted to Heyden's letter of dedication to the Nürnberg patrician Hieronymus Baumgartner, and to an index of chapter headings of the two books that comprise the treatise. Book I treats of the elements of music and Book II is concerned principally with Heyden's theory of *tactus* and mensuration signs.

The modern edition of *De Arte Canendi* endeavors to present a translation of Heyden's text that is accurate and fluent. Heyden's spelling of the names of composers has been retained. Modern equivalents of their names are given in the list of Composers and Compositions, which includes both polyphonic works and individual voice parts that are excerpts of polyphonic pieces. In the text of the treatise Heyden's titles for each composition are given and additional identification is placed in brackets. Names of musical instruments are translated but the original terms are also given. Since the text of *Musicae* 1537 is amplified and extended rather than revised in the edition of 1540, such changes and additions are indicated by footnotes in the modern edition.
Polyphonic works are transcribed into modern notation. Mensuration signs that change within a composition are indicated above the staff. Ligatures and coloration are shown in the usual way.

In *De Arte Canendi* Heyden formulated a theory in which a single unchanging *tactus* is applied to every kind of mensuration sign. This *tactus*-mensuration theory, which is the basis of his work, affirms that the same *tactus* is used for all polyphony in the treatise. The modern transcriptions of the polyphonic pieces are intended to conform to this principle and also to apply his rules of *resolutiones*.

Each transcription has an incipit which shows the original mensuration sign(s). It is essential to observe this sign to determine the tempo intended in the transcription. Heyden considered ○ and 𝄴 as basic mensurations in which a semibreve equals a complete *tactus*. His examples of these mensurations show that a complete *tactus*, which includes many short note values, must move very slowly in order to be sung successfully. On the other hand, his *resolutiones* in 𝄵 are in larger note values and according to him are sung *alla breve*.

[1] For a discussion of *De Arte Canendi* see my article in *Musica Disciplina XXIV* (1970).

In finding a common tempo that accommodates these differences and that also applies Heyden's theories, the following procedure has been adopted: C and O are transcribed with a half note equal to a semibreve. The sign C, for instance, remains a C in transcription and indicates a complete *tactus* of approximately 𝅗𝅥 (◇) = M.M. 36 or a half *tactus* of about ♩ (◇) = M.M. 72. A ¢ used in all voices of a composition is also transcribed with 𝅗𝅥 = ◇, but it retains its modern meaning of ¢, so that in a complete *tactus* a 𝅗𝅥 (◇) = M.M. 72. The sign O is transcribed as $\frac{6}{4}\,\frac{3}{2}$, with the same tempo meaning as C. When multiple mensuration signs are found, as C against ¢, the C is considered as *integer valor*, and the note values under ¢ are halved.

In Ͼ and ⊙ Heyden states that the minim *always* gets the *tactus*, a principle that is also followed in the transcriptions. For example, when Ͼ occurs in all voices the transcription is in $\frac{6}{4}\,\frac{3}{2}$, with a 𝅗𝅥 (◇) equal to M.M. 36 or a complete *tactus*.

The Commentary in this edition discusses a number of the polyphonic examples. Some aspects of Heyden's *tactus*-mensuration theory are also treated with a view to clarifying their meaning.

Grateful acknowledgement is made here to Rev. Walter M. Hayes, S. J., for assistance in Greek passages in *De Arte Canendi*, and to the Stadtbibliothek Nürnberg for a microfilm of Georg Forster's copy of Heyden's treatise.

CLEMENT A. MILLER

COMPOSERS AND COMPOSITIONS

CHAPTER HEADINGS

BOOK I

BOOK II

DE ARTE
CANENDI, AC VERO
SIGNORVM IN CANTIBVS VSV,
libri duo, autore Sebaldo
Heyden.

Ab ipſo authore recogniti, mutati & aucti.

Iſocrates.

ὁρῶμεν τὰς ἐπιδόσεις γινομένας καὶ τῶν τεχνῶν καὶ
τῶν ἄλλων ἁπάντων, οὐ διὰ τοὺς ἐμμένοντας τοῖς καθε-
στῶσιν· ἀλλὰ διὰ τοὺς ἐπανορθοῦντας καὶ τολμῶντας ἀεί
τι κινεῖν, τῶν μὴ καλῶς ἐχόντων.

Norimbergæ apud Ioh. Petreium,
Anno ſalutis M. D. XL.

Cum priuilegio Imp. ad ſexennium

THE ART OF SINGING

Two books by Sebald Heyden on the art of singing and the correct use of signs in songs. Revised and enlarged by the author.

Isocrates [*Evagoras*, 190c]: We know that improvement is made, not only in the arts but also in all other activities, not by those who are satisfied with the establishment, but by those who make corrections and who have the courage constantly to amend whatever may be in need of change.

Printed in Nürnberg by Johannes Petreius in the year of grace, 1540. Rights reserved for six years.

LETTER OF DEDICATION

To the most distinguished Hieronymus Baumgartner, Nürnberg patrician, councillor, and most worthy patron, Sebald Heyden sends heartiest greetings.

Most illustrious sir:

If it is ever true in any matter that afterthoughts are wiser, as they are said to be in the old proverb,[2] it is certainly most true in regard to correcting abuses in customs and arts. This is probably the case because it is very difficult in a first attempt immediately to arrange everything with such exactness and moderation that the result is neither more nor less than the material warrants. Examples in regard to customs are too common to make it necessary to furnish proof here, as when we frequently abolish with violence what could be preserved in some other way, or substitute something else that itself needs correction a little later.

But in restoring liberal arts from abuse and barbarisms to their natural condition and true practice, it is very evident in our times that it is not enough to undertake a work but once and to complete a single attempt, since the difficulty of the subject is so great that in former times it was easier to clean the Augean stable[3] than it is now to restore corrupted arts to their true splendor.

Moreover, I also wonder sometimes who has taken on the greater labor, those who first created these arts or those who are now restoring them. Grammar and dialectics can serve as examples. How many works about them, in what quantities of editions, revisions and amplifications have now seen the light of publication? Yet you can hardly find any authors who do not want to change or enlarge such editions of their own works in some place or other, even in the latest edition. Erasmus of Rotterdam, a most distinguished luminary of scholarship, has left his own testimony: one would no more stop reworking his enriched and more substantial lucubrations than he would stop living.

Since such is the case, why then may I not also hope for indulgence in a similar subject, as I now venture to produce *The Art of Singing and the Correct Use of Musical Signs* in a third edition that is the easiest of all for our youth?

[2] Quoted in Cicero, *Phillipics*, XII, 2, 5: *posteriores enim cogitationes, ut aiunt, sapientiores solent esse.*

[3] *Augiae stabulum repurgare*, a reference to the proverb about Augeas, king of Elis, whose stable, which had not been cleaned in thirty years, was cleaned in one day by Hercules.

For this has always been the sole reason for my labor, as any one easily understands who has carefully compared this works of ours with books on music by any of the older writers, so that it is not at all necessary to hang an ivy branch over our present wine.[4]

All those who have ever made their own attempts in works of a similar nature will easily give credence to me concerning how great a labor it was to collect definite rules on signs from the most diverse examples of various authors, and to restore the former uncertainty and license in the formation of signs to a truly definite science. For such a procedure was necessary, since there is almost no one among older or more recent musicians whose precepts I could really follow.

What, I ask, has Franchinus (otherwise a very careful musician) taught anywhere about the measurement of *tactus* that is comparable to his teaching on proportions with diverse signs, so that our labor might be lightened somewhat? Iohannes Tinctoris, completely occupied with proportional numbers, says too little on signs and nothing at all on the measurement of *tactus*. Georgius Stahlerus, a more recent writer, concerns himself only with giving both the old sign and the true sign to each musical level,[5] (as they say). He could have lightened my present labor in some way if his work had been available to me in sufficient time, for his treatment does not differ much from ours in this book.

I will not say anything about the rest of the later writers, almost all of whom, in any of their works I have seen and read, have preferred to subscribe to the opinions of others rather than to follow the definite judgment of carefully considered reasoning. So it has happened, I believe, that frequently what these writers taught they did not understand themselves. If only those who first created this art had left us not only examples but also books of precepts! For in this way our own divination would have been less necessary, especially since their era is not so far removed from our time, so that, like the tradition of the [Guidonian] hand, their writings would not have been lost to such an extent, just as their musical examples have been preserved.

I believe there are many things which indicate that the invention of musical figures as presently constituted is not so old, but that it occurred a little before the memory of men of our time. In the first place, almost no polyphonic musical compositions are found anywhere which are proven to be more than one hundred years old. In addition, it is well known that older musicians, as Boethius, Capella, and the like, have taught absolutely nothing about our present art of singing, so that we cannot easily understand what their music was like; also, if they ever concerned themselves with our kind of music they certainly have not stated it.

I am speaking here about that music which harmonizes and unites as if into one body so many types of varied notes, so many proportions of diverse

[4] A reference to a maxim attributed to Publilius Syrus: you need not hang an ivy branch over wine that will sell.

[5] *i. e.*, to *modus, tempus, prolatio.*

signs, with so many voices that are variously placed but completely consonant in their harmonious accord. Georgius Forsterus, an expert in literature and medicine as well as in music, recently made available to me the work on proportions by Iohannes Tinctoris, in which he calls this kind of music a new art, and states that it was first created in England by a certain Dunstaple, and then given greater renown by the Frenchmen Dufay and Binchois, and finally it became more and more illustrious in the hands of Iohannes Okgekhem, Busnois, and Caron.

Although this art is new and completely unknown to ancient Greek writers, it will be no less admired and praised than any of the oldest arts, unless perhaps through envy we refuse to give it a place of glory among the inventions of our times, while if it had been invented by the ancients they would have honored and revered it as a revelation from heaven. But then, what invention of the ancients is there with which the art of printing books in our times, invented by Germans, could not contend for glory?

So much is still lacking in our music that its newness should be neither honored nor despised, especially if one considers thoughtfully that just as skill and acumen are needed to express in writing the fluency and flexibility of a language, so also are they necessary in the same degree to combine diverse musical intervals into a fully consonant harmony; again, just as they are needed to place an entire text with its characteristic shapes or figures before the eyes so clearly and so definitely that whatever is read or spoken is understood merely by ordinary letters of the alphabet, so also what should be sung, how much a tone should be raised or lowered, lengthened or shortened, is understood by notes and signs. And assuredly, if one examines closely examples of the first *componistae* (for they have left us only a written art), he will be amazed at their extreme carefulness in demonstrating the things that pertain to the artistic manipulation of tone, either in definite figures or colors, or signs, or numbers; they did this with no less ability and skill than did any of the grammarians in whatever they prescribed for variety in speech, so that music also, through manifold variety, possesses its own charm in accordance with the pleasing talents of its composers.

If this ability is evident anywhere, it is surely revealed and demonstrated very beautifully in the compositions of Iohannes Ghiselinus and Iacobus Obertus.[6] The former, in *Missa Gratieusa* (a work given special attention in this book), has presented in planned examples, as if in a mirror, whatever he considered worthy of understanding in regard to signs. The latter, in his *Ienedemande*,[7] has repeatedly played about with changes of signs as varied as they are artful, so that in the examples and testimonies of these two men a definite relationship of signs would always be evident if the hidden meaning of the signs were revealed by a prescribed limit in the art, not by the accidental introduction of varying kinds of *tactus*.

[6] Jacob Obrecht.

[7] *Je ne demande.*

Through this accident of changing the *tactus* the relationship and nature of all proportions having mutually dissimilar signs are confused and defective. Indeed, how unnecessary it was to invent so many different kinds of *tactus* that even now we endure unwillingly! For when we see many kinds of *tactus* invented simply to change the tempo of a composition frequently, making it now slower, now faster, and now very fast, then I ask, what are we to think later composers (*novatores*) understood by proportions, augmentations and diminutions? From the art itself it is absolutely certain that they wanted to show through various kinds of *tactus* the same thing that early composers (*veteres*) had indicated more correctly and artistically either by a diminution of signs or by proportions.

Thus, if the inventors of the art inscribed a song with complete (*integra*) signs, they wanted this meaning kept without fail, so that the harmonies could move along as complete accords and with a certain reserve. If they added diminution, however, they either intersected the circles with a vertical line or introduced a proportion of *genus multiplex* in order to accelerate the song, so that, as if hurrying, it would hasten to the end. This undoubtedly happened because in diminished signs one *tactus* contained as many of the same note values as two *tactus* in an *integer* sign. Also in *proportio tripla* one *tactus* contained as many of the same note values as three *tactus* in an *integer* sign. Thus it was entirely unnecessary for later writers to create more *tactus* in a song in order to get faster or slower, especially since it is wholly incongruous in any art to teach with many rules and precepts what can be taught very correctly and clearly with one rule.

It is strange, therefore, that this point was not considered by musicians of a little earlier time, namely: many kinds of *tactus* cannot occur in a relation of proportions, but of necessity only one and the same kind of unchanging *tactus*. They could have discovered this very easily from the agreement of the various proportions, for they were never able to sing concordantly a complete *tactus* in *integer*, a diminished *tactus* in *dupla*, and a proportionate *tactus* in *tripla*, so that from all thoroughly disguised varieties of *tactus* they were inevitably compelled to choose one certain kind, and it alone, regardless of the diversity of the proportions. We will now demonstrate this with a similar case.

If some current arithmetician, in teaching computations, introduced many species of the unit one (*monas*) that were mutually different in quantity, and compared them to other numbers in proportions, what, I ask, has he done other than to obscure not only the entire ratio and rule of the proportions, but also to create a relationship that was plainly insoluble? But since musical signs are clearly nothing else but the very notes of proportions, notes which must be referred to a definite *tactus*, as if to the unit one, what sort of thanks do we owe those musicians who have produced many mutually divergent kinds of *tactus*? For in this way they have obscured and confused the nature of signs and their proportional agreement to such an extent that they themselves could hardly know anything definite about the subject, much less teach it to others. Or if they really did know anything, they learned it from practice alone, not from the art, so that when questioned they cannot prove their opinion with a genuine reason.

So it happens that, just as you do not find a single word among the older and better teachers of the art of music concerning different kinds of *tactus*, also among the more recent writers you see nothing really definite taught about mutually comparable musical signs. The reason is, as we previously stated, that in creating so many kinds of *tactus* they made a matter otherwise clear in itself confused and almost insoluble.

It is little wonder, therefore, that even while certain writers discuss musical signs in an inept fashion, others consider them to be entirely superfluous and without value to the art. Since they do not see the true relationship of the signs, it is easy for them to make light of this ignorance and to say: it does not matter that various signs are written in songs, since there is only one formula, or possibly two, according to which all types of songs can be written most correctly. Also, the mere writing of diverse signs does not result from any art, but it is just as if one would write the text of a speech by using now these words or phrases, now those, so that in their common formula there would still be enough familiar words. This is what they say.

But in the same way, why do they not state that no variety may exist in the Latin language for the sake of a more copious style, but that everything should rather be tautological? Or that they own no additional clothes, since they could constantly wear a single garment, and a very simple one at that, just as though they could recognize the value or length of any notes without observing their special signs? Then let them compose a song to which no sign is prefixed, and let them answer how much each breve, or long, or even semibreve is worth. But possibly they will guess or infer from the polyphonic texture what must be sung and in what way. They really speak nobly!

But it would be remarkable if this uncertainty about the mensuration of a song, in addition to the more laborious search for its note values through the harmony, did not rather frequently discourage their weary minds from the study of singing, or at least make them ashamed when they try to discover the value of notes from the harmony alone, without signs. Only a few, however, have that ability; whoever desires it must understand the art of composition. But then, among a hundred present-day singers who consider themselves excellent, you find hardly one or other who knows the art so well that he dares to profess himself a teacher of singing.

Therefore, we consider the use of signs so necessary that we contend nobody can truly understand the art of singing without investigating and observing them very diligently. But while we say that the use of signs supports the entire art of singing, some may pretend that their use means nothing. For although the entire art of singing consists of varied note shapes and their differing values, and notes become now longer, now shorter, through various proportions, their frequent change of value must have its own definite indications or necessary signs without which they could not be investigated, much less even observed.

Surely we may deservedly censure those scoffers who glibly assert that ability in singing is an art, but who meanwhile reject and deny a principal constituent of the art.

This is no different than if one proclaims that construction in wood or in stone is an art, but contends that such items as carpenters' squares, red ochre, rulers, plumb-lines and the like are unnecessary because through chance effort all the work can be finished. But if this were really so, what kind of structures can we expect at completion? How skilfully are walls joined with joists? How accurately are columns erected? But if it were not so, as when columns stand at an angle, when longer and shorter beams do not fit together, when the size of the roof in proportion to the foundation does not agree at all, so that the unskillfully made structure collapses?

In my opinion exactly the same thing happens in musical compositions in which no signs are written, or at least are not written accurately enough. It is easy to see, when one singer begins in a validly quicker tempo and another follows in an equally valid slower tempo, that the entire musical structure will collapse and the musical harmony will turn into gutteral grunts. Yet there is a certain dissimilarity in our comparison, for when a poorly made structure collapses onto its foundation, its crashing descent is thoroughly frightening, and those inside the structure are very often crushed; on the contrary, if poorly organized music in a celebrated choir begins to fall apart at its joints through unskilled or inattentive singers, it hardly ever causes fright among any of the relatively undisturbed listeners, but nearly always provokes laughter. Nobody ever expires, unless perhaps one or two listeners (for a few can still be found), who in their greater understanding of the art mourn an undertaking not worthy enough to have been blessed with success.

In summary, signs in a song are the notes of proportions. But the nature and the variety of songs consist in their own definite proportions. Therefore, whoever says that signs mean nothing, or contends that they can be omitted, plainly destroys whatever meaning music has as an art.

These, then, are the things I wished especially to fulfil in our books. First, to make the art of singing as easy and expeditious as possible for young students. Second, to return the value and use of signs to definite proportional relationships, so that in any examination one may immediately understand their use and value. I leave the reader to judge with fairness and justice to what extent I may have attained each of these aims, promising myself only that even if I do not satisfy everyone, there still will be almost no one to whom my diligence and honesty in this matter is objectionable.

It is indeed evident that in some examples which are not mine but which were acquired from others to demonstrate the rules, I have changed the form of the notes, or in some other examples I have placed the note forms with different signs, applying a form other than that used by the composer himself. In this I have no doubt that any fair judge will believe it was done for a proper and just reason, because, despite the changes in notes and signs, the nature of a song is entirely complete and unchanged in what pertains to contrapuntal composition and the intent of the composer, and it always remains unaltered. Moreover, this can be defended with just reasons, partly because the somewhat older musical structure is more pleasing to my spirit, and partly to give chirping young boys (I like to speak so) a specimen, as it were, of the manifold variety of mensural music, in which it is very easy to transcribe any song, even if changed ten times from one form to another. This is done with such equity that no composer can complain it has been the cause of any harm to him. Yet we have done this scarcely once or twice, and only in demonstration of simple rules which are totally uncontroversial, for we were aware that original and perfect examples must be used in controversies and confutations.

I was glad to mention these points here of my own accord and in anticipation, as it were, so that some dilettante does not attack through malice and calumny such an example he may discover accidentally, and claim that falsehoods were substituted for truth.

Possibly I could have treated more briefly what pertains to the order and disposition of our present labor if I had been free to use fewer examples. But since this art is based no less on practice than on precepts, or rather I should say that it demands longer time devoted to practice than to precepts, I did not wish to leave anything lacking to our youth in this respect, especially since these examples, from which true art can be learned, are not met with everywhere, and when they are, they still can hardly be understood by anyone without knowledge of their precepts.

I now dedicate once again my current labor, of whatever kind it may be, to your excellence, my dear friend Baumgartner, so that it may appear in public under the felicitous auspices of your name. I see no one whom this present edition could have as a more suitable patron, because you have joined an admirable humanity with literary erudition in such a way that it is very difficult to know whether to praise you more for humaneness or for learning, in particular because of your remarkable benevolence toward liberal arts and scholars pursuing them. The fact that liberal arts, held in such contempt and a stranger in the midst of crass materialism, still has any place here is due in large measure to you, so that it is because of your merit that all men of learning wish to praise and extol you with every kind of honor.

Most worthy patron, you are also related to this art of ours because you too love the art of music with singular devotion, and because of the same bond Ludovicus Senflius, principal composer at present in all Germany, is known to you not only as an acquaintance but in a truly close friendship. I would gladly have used the counsel and judgment of this man in my books if I had been acquainted with him before the present time, but I, as a stranger to him (a great regret to me), could never cause concern to someone unknown to me. To be sure, several times I sought a meeting with him through relatives[8] of mine who know him rather well, but through some unknown inconvenience it has not

[8] *i. e., affines,* relatives by marriage.

gone beyond this point, so that my wish has not been granted. But regardless of that, in the German Ludovicus Senflius I honor and extol the excellence of German music, for I am far from ever wishing that praise of him in my books should not be greatly increased rather than neglected.

But I now return to you, most distinguished Sir, praying over and over that in your kindness you will benignly accept my current work once again dedicated to you, in place of the small gifts that friends usually interchange every January 1st, and that you will allow it a place in your library as a token of my love for you. Your Sebald promises you that he will never neglect what he knows to depend for its own worth on honoring your virtues. A sincere belief also sustains me that you will never be lacking in counsel and assistance to my children, if perchance you outlive me (God grant it) and any of them needs your patronage to pursue his literary studies; then may they have security from you, with whom, twenty years from now, they may remember the exhausting labor of their father in the schools of our community.

For in your wisdom you are aware that the memory of accomplished good deeds grows old very quickly, especially in the field of education. As things are now it can almost be said that there is no one who does not think that anything spent on teachers and those engaged in philosophy, even if it is less than adequate, is still excessive and more than they deserve.

Farewell, T. D., through Christ the Lord, from the Sebaldine study, on January 1, in the year of Christ 1540.

BOOK I

Music, that is, the Art of Singing

PREFACE

We have learned through experience that a far different method of instruction is needed to teach untutored boys than to train those who have been taught carefully for some time. In the same way, we know that in a statuary workshop far different tools are used to hew out rough pieces than to polish the product later. For just as in hewing rough pieces there are appropriately heavier pick-axes which penetrate more forcibly and cut off the original roughness, so also the roughness of youthful natures demands a certain more straightforward lucidity in teaching.

It seemed here that such lucidity would be shown most suitably if to certain rather brief questions I gave in answer the precepts to be taught, and did so in specific and definitive terms, just as in a dialog; and finally, adding individual examples for each of the precepts, so that young boys would grasp very easily whatever is being taught, just as they do in counting on their fingers. Therefore, let those who so desire make use of these precepts, however constituted; may they also consider my work fairly, in which I have attempted to be of the utmost benefit to untutored youth.

CHAPTER 1

What is music?

It is the art of producing tones correctly and melodiously, and in this way it pertains to sound. Music is produced in three ways: by the human voice, by wind instruments (*fistulae*), and by string instruments. Voices create sound by movement of the tongue, wind instruments by blowing, and string instruments by striking.

What is the origin of music?

It comes from the muses, whom the ancients revered as guardians of the liberal arts, undoubtedly because with this name they meant to show a certain quickening of the human spirit influenced by divine authority, as well as a zeal for studies, qualities that are also highly necessary in a modern authority who teaches liberal arts. And this is why the muses are considered to be daughters of Jove and Memoria, and derive their names ἀπὸ τοῦ μῶσθαι, that is, from seeking[9], or ἁπὸ τοῦ μάσαι, that is, from teaching.

[9] In Plato's *Cratylus*, 406a, the muses are named παρὰ τὸ μαίεθαι from searching, and also from philosophy; in Isadore's *Etymologiarum* III, 15, 1, muses are named ἀπὸ τοῦ μυεῖθαι, *id est a quarendo*.

How many kinds of music are there?

Two kinds are usually treated: plainsong (*musica choralis*) and mensural music (*musica figurata*). What is plainchant? It is music in which a simple and almost uniform note-shape of one color always retains the same value, excluding any augmentation or diminution. Examples are songs used daily in churches.

What is mensural music?

It is music in which various notes with differing shapes, colors, and prefixed signs, repeatedly change value. Nothing in particular is taught here about plainchant, for it is not necessary, since it has the same kind of scale and solmization as mensural music. Thus, whoever understands mensural music properly will also understand plainsong.

What is the use of the art of singing?

It is used for the recreation of students of liberal arts or others occupied with serious activities, to lighten the weariness born of labor and to refresh men exhausted from continued application. For music has a truly singular power to please, in that it dispels a feeling of weariness and maintains one's enthusiasm for work. We use it in the same way that we normally use sleep and similar inactivity, that is, whenever we have completed some burdensome and serious matters. For while almost the only function of music may be to please the sensibilities of listeners, yet it is never fitting for a wise person to revel in pleasure, but only to make use of it.

Therefore, those who have completely neglected all serious studies and who devote themselves entirely to song and the cultivation of musical instruments, as if they were destined by nature for good times alone, are deservedly considered foolish.[10] In the same way we believe persons are very stupid who devote themselves so completely to sleep and relaxation that they never think of awakening and carrying on any of the more necessary activities.

If the practice of music has no philosophical basis and makes no contribution to more serious studies, it is never worthy but always tends to error, as Ovid attests: Citharas and songs and lyres enervate the mind, and the voice and arms moving in their own rhythm.[11]

So we generally see that men who prate about nothing but dancing, lovemaking, and adultery, have gone from boyhood to maturity in schools for entertainers (*ludiones*) without studying any serious discipline. But there are also those so unphilosophical that their use of music makes them temperamental and unreasonable rather than mild-mannered, and this happens all the more that they consider themselves more outstanding in this art. For how many remarkable harpists and lutenists[12] are there who are not also remarkably afflicted with

[10] It is possible that Heyden was influenced by Erasmus, who decried the lack of learning and morals in many singers. In *De Arte Canendi* Heyden calls Erasmus a *clarissimum rei literariae lumen.* For Erasmus's views on music see Clement A. Miller, "Erasmus on Music", *The Musical Quarterly LII* (1966).

[11] *Enervant animos Citharae, Cantusque, Lyraeque / Et vox et numeris brachia mota suis,* from *Remedia Amoris,* 753.

[12] For these instrumentalists Heyden wrote *citharoedi* and *fidicines.*

this churlish fault, so that "when asked to play by friends they never want to, but when not asked they never stop"?[13]

So what praise do they merit, who can correct with the greatest keenness the smallest discrepancies in tuning their strings, yet who meanwhile allow the course of their life to be utterly discordant through every kind of fault? But we could very easily correct these faults if we would teach our young boys to play instruments and at the same time would also teach the precepts of philosophical disciplines and any other honest studies we want them to imbibe. The result would be that their minds, fortified as it were by more weighty studies, would be correspondingly less softened by the spell of music or harden into arrogantly insensible ways.

But if one or other must be chosen, what sane person does not prefer some serious discipline to skill in playing woodwind and string instruments, especially since everywhere a great many entertainers are found who sing or dance lasciviously for gratuities and who make themselves ridiculous to thoughtful men? On the other hand, if the occasion demanded it, very few of them could be thoughtful or wise. A proverb of our country says prudently and correctly: every upright man must be most careful that he knows entertainers rather than that they know him.

We do not write these things to censure the very beautiful art of singing, but rather to liberate it from the idle enticements of entertainers and strolling players (*errones*) and to restore it to its true function, in which it may serve to please not so much the idle tastes of epicures as those who foster liberal arts and true virtue.

What, is there no use of music in churches?

There is certainly some, but it is used not so much during the solemn parts of the service as for the cultivation of spiritual thoughts. For God is not worshiped by sounds and bells but by a true heart and soul, so that in divine worship there is no need for a strong voice, but rather for a more collected spirit.[14] St. Paul says: speak to one another in psalms, hymns, and spiritual songs, singing and making melody in your hearts to the Lord. Ephesians 5. On this account we also use church music as a spiritual exercise after we have prayed to the Lord in more serious and grave rites.

How many accidentals are necessary to the art of singing?

Eight: scale, key, *tactus*, notes, dots, rests, mensurations, Tones.

CHAPTER 2

Scales, Keys and their use

What is a scale?

It is an arrangement of straight lines and equidistant spaces by which we dis-

[13] Adapted by Heyden from Horace's *Satires*, I, 3, 1, in which the reference is to singers.

[14] A similar sentiment was voiced by Erasmus: let us sing sparingly, but let us sing more in our hearts. Miller, *op. cit.*, p. 339.

tinguish the inscribed notes in every kind of song. In Greek it is called a system.

What is the reason for observing lines and spaces in a song?

So that through the distance between them the rise and fall of notes (which are the signs of tones) are quickly and accurately perceived. For if notes were written on an unlined surface no one could tell with certainty how much a tone should rise or fall. But if parallel lines are added, the intervals between notes are seen at first glance.

Why do musicians use the term scale?

As far as can be conjectured there are two reasons for this appellation. First, from its shape, since parallel lines so inscribed with notes represent in a certain way the transverse wooden steps (called κλιμακτηρὲς in Greek) of ladders. The second reason appears to be taken from practice, for the letters or keys of a musical ladder are named in exactly the same way as one ascends or descends the steps of a ladder.

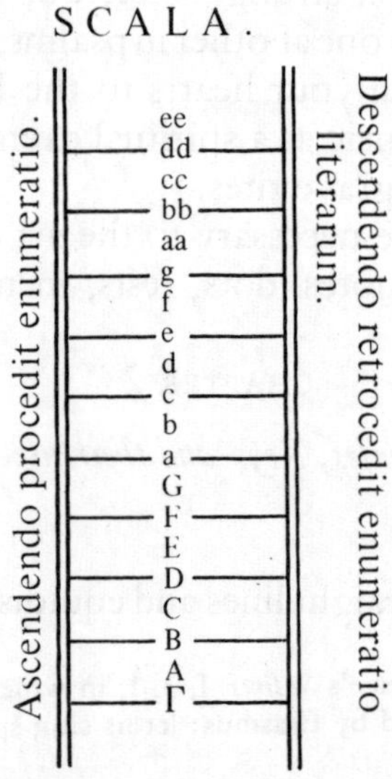

What are the keys?

Keys are these seven letters: *a b c d e f g*. When they are applied to the scale system three times, one to each line and space, they determine the highness or lowness of a human tone. For the entire meaning of the art of music depends on whether one knows how far a tone should ascend or descend, since one does not sing if he constantly produces the same tone. Singing, therefore, is nothing else than the ability to raise or lower a musical tone in accordance with the needs of the vocal material.

Old musicians taught the rise and fall of a tone very clearly through the monochord, a one-stringed instrument with a string of predetermined length stretched between two bridges. On the flat board under the bridge intervals from the lowest to the highest are marked with definite intersections. When the moveable lower bridge is gradually brought upward and the string is plucked at each intersection, all ascending intervals are produced very exactly. In the same way, if you lower the bridge all descending intervals are formed.

So that young boys may understand this procedure more accurately we will let them produce the sound by hand and so experience it by ear. Because of the shortness of the page the line adjoined on the right is in two sections, and constitutes a representation of a complete string with its definite divisions. If a boy marks it on the soundboard of a lute, under the fifth string, as they say, and places a bridge at each end, by moving one bridge forward and backward step by step he will hear very clearly which keys are correct and what intervals occur between them.

Examples of this line or monochord are found in all kinds of musical instruments. On harps (*citharae*) and clavichords (*clavichorda*), as they are usually called, the different strings are the same as different divisions of the monochord. Since on a monochord many divisions cannot be sounded at the same time, the necessities of the matter compelled many strings to be developed from one string, just as the formation of counterpoint, as they say, demanded many simultaneous consonant sounds. In the same way boys should understand that frets on the necks of lutes and finger holes on pipes are nothing but particular measurements of this monochord.

Fulcrum superius immobile

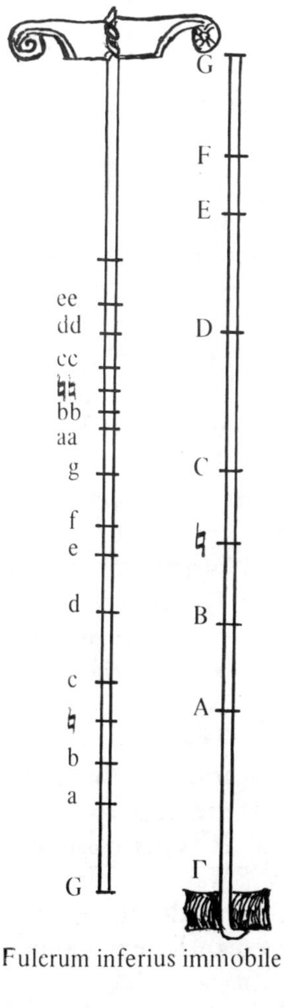

Fulcrum inferius immobile.

How many keys of a system or monochord are there?

With regard to sound alone there are twenty-three keys on a monochord, as we have shown in the previous diagram. But since they follow an order of position and not of sound, they number only twenty, doubtless because in performing songs the sounds of *b fa* ♮ *mi* differ, yet they always occupy the same place. The following diagram shows the order and names of the keys.

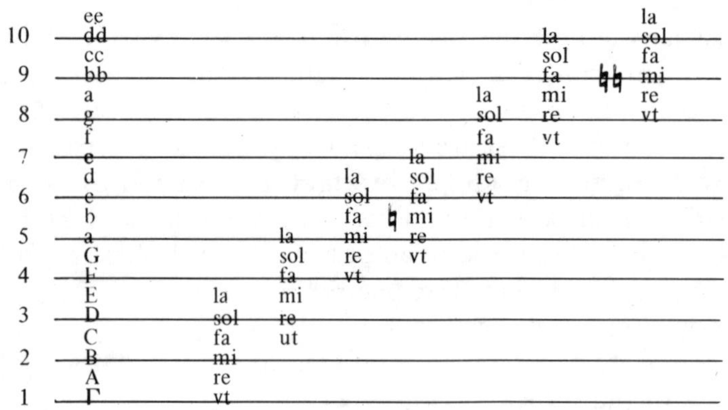

Why are letters of a system called keys?

Because they open specified melodies and indeed the system's entire range of songs, so to speak, and expose them to the eyes, just as the key of a bookcase, when inserted in a lock and turned, immediately reveals any contents that had previously been concealed.

How are the keys of a system divided?

Into low, median, and high.

Which are low keys?

The eight low capital letters: *Γ, A, B, C, D, E, F, G.* They are called low because in songs in which they are found they are usually sung in a deep and full tone. Singers call this voice-part the bass.

Which are median keys?

The seven small letters: *a, b, c, d, e, f, g.* They are called median because they form the middle range between deep, low tones and high tones. We hear this range in the concord of tenor and alto, as they are called.

Which are the high keys?

The five highest and doubled letters: *aa, bb, cc, dd, ee,* which form the thinnest and highest sound, such as children produce. We usually call this part the *discantus*.

It is permissible to add to the usual twenty keys?

Why not? It is even necessary when a song exceeds its upper or lower limit. But in adding new keys one must be careful to maintain the order of the seven median letters and syllables. Young students will find this treated later among examples of solmization, for the second example[15] rises to *gg sol re ut*, and the tenth[16] descends a perfect fourth below *Γ ut*.

What then is the use of keys placed on each step of lines and spaces of the scale?

It is twofold. First, to indicate definite interval sizes, so that the distance between various tones may be recognized by the order of the letters alone. Intervals will be taught a little later. Second, so that in the order of keys, as in an arithmetic table, in a mirror so to speak, young boys may recognize with the greatest ease and certainty the basis of any song, doubtless because the staff lines which are seen in every song are a definite part of the aforementioned system. For notes placed on certain lines and spaces and characteristic keys written at the beginning of songs are no different than those signs shown in their respective positions in the foregoing system, so that one knows immediately which keys belong to which notes.

What are characteristic keys (*claves characteristicae*)?

They are keys in certain shapes that are written only at the beginning of a song, while all the other keys, including their letters, as if concealed, are understood mentally and are not seen with the eyes.

How many characteristic keys are there?

There are five, *F*, *c*, *g*, ♭, ♮. In every song they are placed on certain staff lines at the beginning of each line of music. *Γ ut* and *dd la sol* are also counted among characteristic keys, but we have omitted them here, for it does not seem necessary to indicate them.

What are the shapes of the characteristic keys?

They vary according to the kind of song. In plainsong the letters *F*, *c*, *g*, are simply written, and in mensural music): or 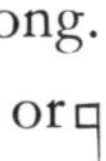 are used for *F*, and  for *c*; *g* is the same in both, and is always a small letter.

What are the uses of characteristic keys?

They are twofold. The letters *f*, *c*, *g*, indicate their position in the system, but round ♭ and square ♮ show the quality of a song according to the use of soft ♭ or hard ♮. Thus, when any one of the three letters, *f*, *c*, *g*, is placed at the beginning of a song, young boys can instantly recognize the system's position through it, since a line on which a characteristic key is placed in a song is always the same line that this key occupies in the system. Moreover, all keys and lines above and below are shown in songs in exactly the same order as they are arranged in the system. The following formulas are a very clear demonstration.

[15] Ex. 3 of the polyphonic examples.
[16] Ex. 11.

Pars Systematis acuta.

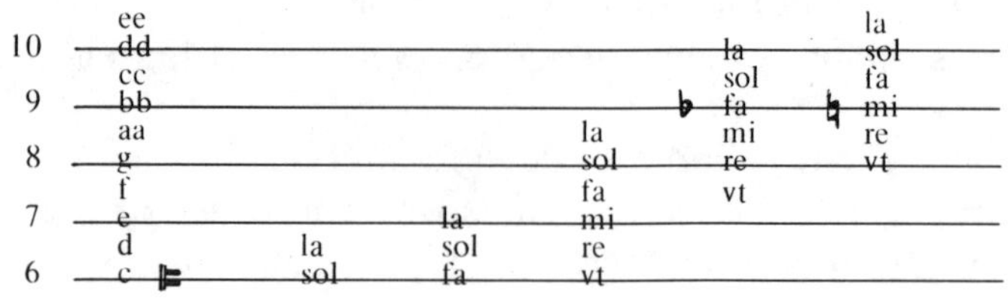

Pars Systematis media.

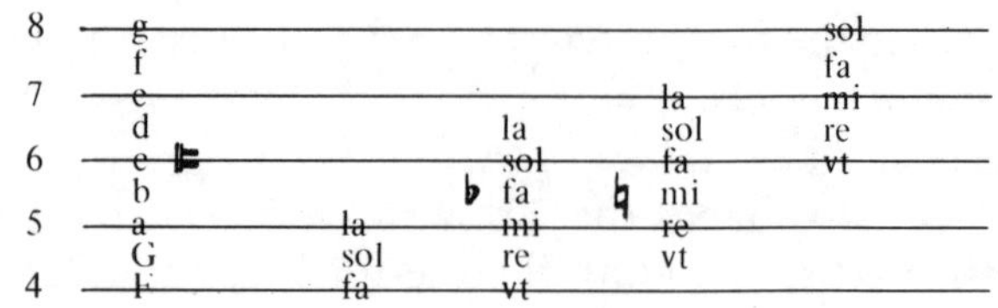

Pars Systematis grauis.

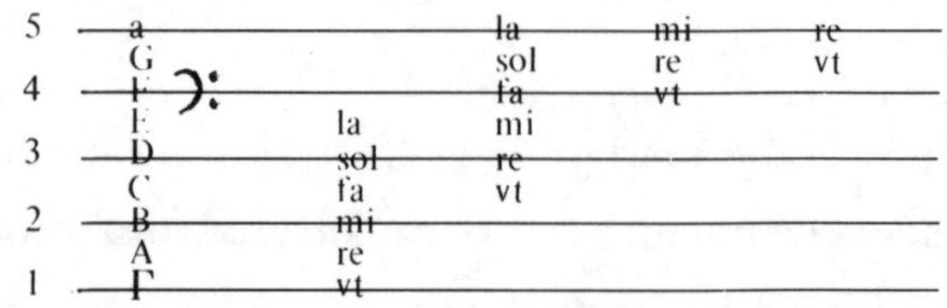

Vocables

What is the use of vocables selected for application on each key in the system?

Their reciprocal use allows us to assign to every song its proper and specific melody, for these syllables are nothing else than specific names of intervals. There are six of them: *ut*, *re*, *mi*, *fa*, *sol*, *la*. The following song shows their interrelated order.

Canon at the fifth below.

Ex. 1 [*Benedictus* from *Missa L'homme arme sexti toni* — Josquin des Prez]

How are these vocables divided?

We divide them into upper and lower vocables. We call the lower ones *ut, re, mi*; if, on keys of two or three vocables, they cannot continue upward through *fa, sol, la,* as far as necessary, then they usually substitute for the missing vocables. We call the upper ones *fa, sol, la*; in the same way they substitute for lower vocables whenever in keys of two or three vocables they cannot be lowered through *mi, re, ut,* as far as the lower melody requires. How much this situation differs from the rules of solmization students will see more clearly later, providing that they have previously learned about musical intervals.

CHAPTER 3

Intervals

What is an interval?

An interval is the distance by which a tone is raised or lowered.

How many musical intervals are there?

There are as many intervals as can be formed from the distance of one tone to another higher or lower tone. But in order to accommodate the subject to young students a few of the common intervals are listed here: unison, semitone, whole tone, minor third, major third, perfect fourth, perfect fifth, minor sixth, major sixth, minor seventh, major seventh, octave. In studying these intervals I believe youthful minds should consider not so much their exact size on a monochord as the order of the six vocables and the ordinary scale's lines and spaces as seen in every song. In this way they will understand and retain all intervals more easily and fully.

What is a unison?

It is a tone which retains the same pitch and which does not rise or fall. All notes on the same line or space are called unisons. Therefore, a unison is not an interval, but a basis of other intervals which should be related to it.

What is a semitone?

It is an interval which ascends from *mi* to *fa*, or descends from *fa* to *mi*.

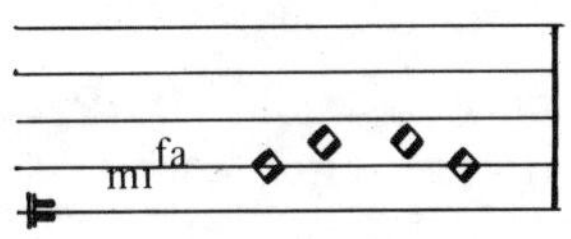

What is a whole tone (*tonus*)?

It is the movement of a tone from a line to the next space or from a space to the next line, as *ut* to *re*, *re* to *mi*, *fa* to *sol*, *sol* to *la*, and the reverse, excepting the semitone *mi fa*.

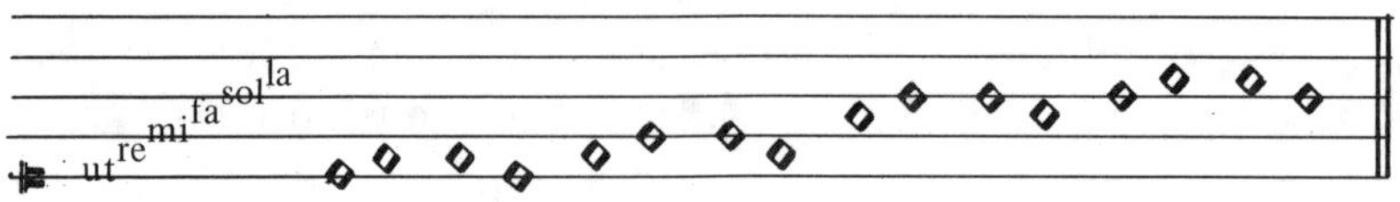

What is a minor third (*semiditonus*)?

It is the interval of a line to the next line or a space to the next space in which a minor third is contained, as *re* to *fa*, *mi* to *sol*. It is usually called a minor third (*tertia minor*), because a whole tone and a semitone are contained within three scale steps.

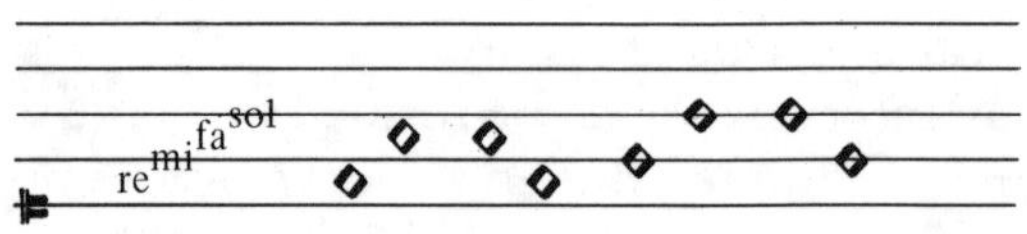

What is a major third (*ditonus*)?

It is the interval of a line to the next line or a space to the next space in which no semitone is contained, as *ut* to *mi*, *fa* to *la*. It is usually called a major third (*tertia maior*), because two whole tones are contained within three scale steps.

What is a perfect fourth (*diatessaron*)?

It is an interval leap from a line to the second space or from a space to the second line, in which the two tones are mutually consonant, as *ut* to *fa*, *re* to *sol*, and *mi* to *la*. Some call it a fourth because two whole tones and one semitone are contained within four scale steps.

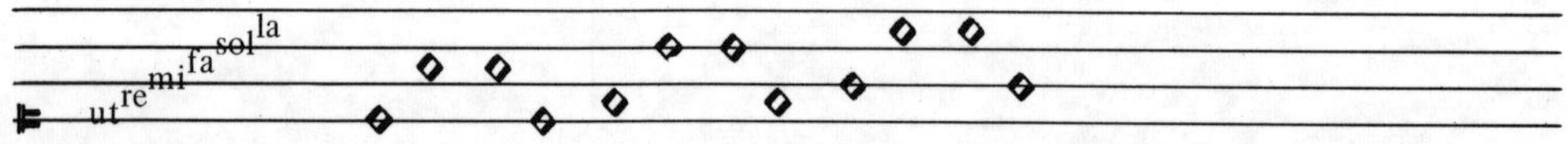

What is a perfect fifth (*diapente*)?

It is an interval leap from a line to the third line or from a space to the third space, as *ut* to *sol*, *re* to *la*, *mi* to *mi*, and *fa* to *fa*. It is usually called a fifth because it ascends or descends five scale steps.

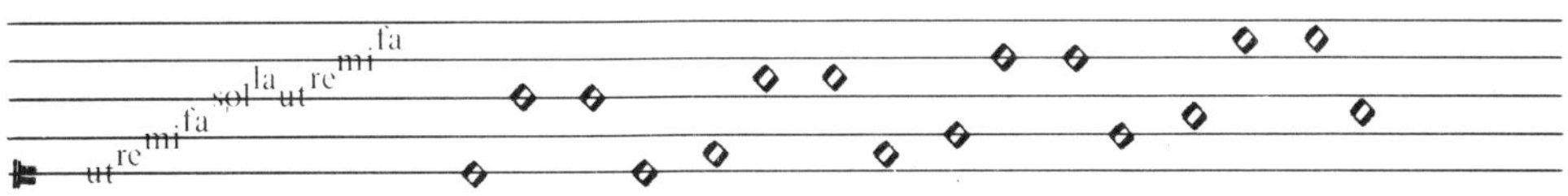

What is a minor sixth (*semitonium cum diapente*)?

It is an interval leap from a line to the third space or from a space to the third line, and it contains two semitones and three whole tones. An example is *mi fa* sung at the beginning and end of a sixth. Singers usually call it a minor sixth (*sexta minor*) because two semitones are included in six scale steps.

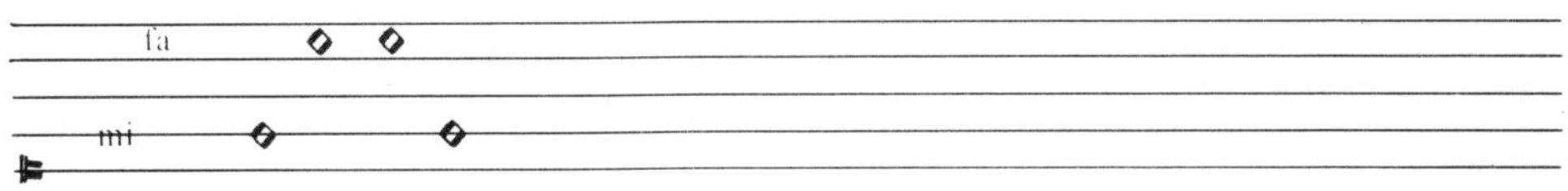

What is a major sixth (*tonus cum diapente*)?

It is an interval leap from a line to the third space or from a space to the third line in which four whole tones and only one semitone are contained. An example is *ut* to *la* a sixth away. It is also called a major sixth (*sexta maior*) because it contains only one semitone between six scale steps.

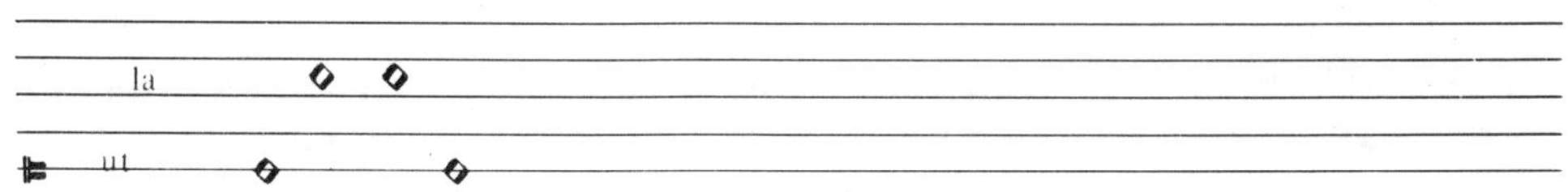

What is a minor seventh (*semitonus cum diapente*)?

It is an interval leap from a space to a fourth space or from a line to a fourth line in which two semitones and four whole tones are contained. It is usually called a minor seventh (*septima minor*). Examples are *ut mi* and *re fa*, because seven ascending or descending steps are counted between the paired vocables.[17]

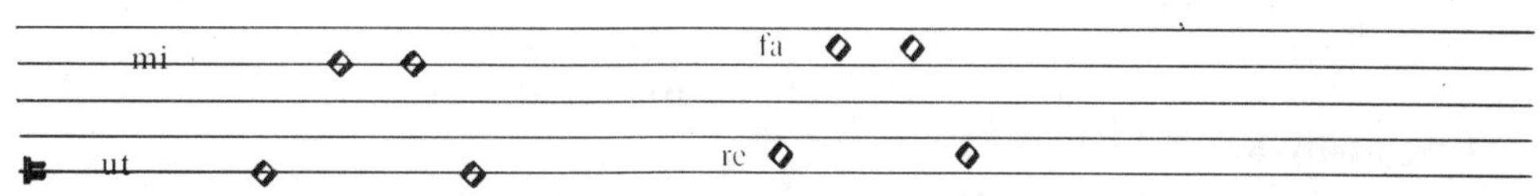

[17] The first seventh, *ut mi*, is of course a major and not a minor seventh. It is difficult to explain Heyden's error on this point.

His musical example also illustrates both sevenths. In the 1537 edition the syllables *ut mi* are lacking in the text, making the definition correct. *Musicae* of 1532 defines both sevenths correctly.

What is an octave (*diapason*)?

It is an interval leap from a line to a fourth space or from a space to a fourth line. It is called an octave (*diapason*) because it includes all intervals discussed thus far and reverts to itself as it were. It is also called an octave (*octavus*) because its interval size contains eight scale steps.

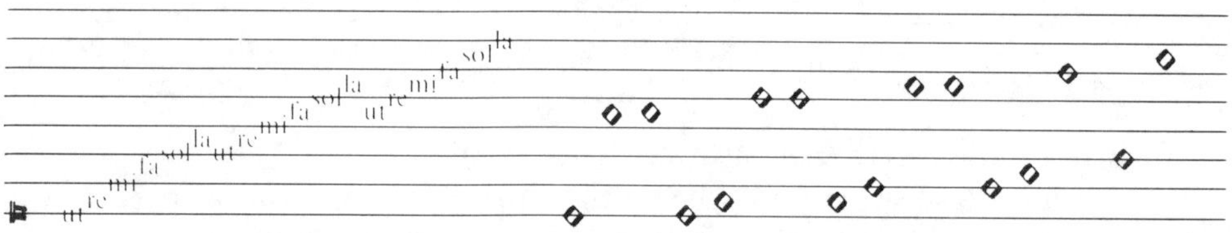

There are many other intervals which are usually numbered so: if a tone or semitone is added to an octave, they form a ninth; if a major or minor third is added, a tenth; if a perfect fourth is added, an eleventh; if a perfect fifth is added, a twelfth. But we merely wanted to mention these intervals here and not to discuss them, because they can be learned in time through practice rather than rule.

CHAPTER 4

Solmization, as it is called, or the naming of tones

What is solmization (*solmifatio*)?

It is the appropriate and expeditious use of vocables adjoined to all keys for varied melodic formations.

How many things are necessary to learn solmization speedily and accurately?

There are two. First: before starting, singers should memorize very carefully the system shown earlier[18] with its keys and vocables and also its proper numbers, so to speak, and apply them to the beginning of each song. In this way they will truly understand the constitution of all songs placed before them. Second: they should carefully observe through *b fa* and ♮ *mi*, as principal keys in all songs, the use and movement of vocables and tones of all other keys. For nobody can sing any song accurately and dependably unless first he has expressly considered *b fa* ♮ *mi* and then decides where *mi* or *fa* should be applied. It is most important to know whether *mi* or *fa* is sung on *b fa* ♮ *mi*, since either of them influences the special nature and quality of a melody. It is because of this that several kinds of hexachords[19] are enumerated.

How many kinds of hexachords are there?

There are three: natural, soft *b*, and hard ♮. To these some have added a fourth, called *fictus*. But for the sake of an easier method of teaching we have

[18] The diagram on p. 30

[19] For the word hexachord Heyden does not use *hexachordum* or *deductio*, but *cantus*, and sometimes also *cantio*.

decided that only two, soft *b* and hard ♮ are enough since every song either does or does not have *b* written at the beginning.

What is the soft *b* hexachord?

It is one which has *b* written at the beginning and which arranges the tones of all the other keys above and below according to *b fa*. This is the case if *b fa* keeps its position directly below *c sol fa ut*, for if a prescribed *b* occupies a different place it will make *cantus fictus*, in which regular scale tones are neglected and other substitute tones are formed, so that *mi*, *re*, *ut* will fit below *fa* written on *b*, and *sol la* will fit above it. Such hexachords are not determined by any other key than *b*. Thus we do not wish to separate them from a soft *b* hexachord, since they depend entirely on a prescribed *b*.

What is the hard ♮ hexachord?

It is one which has no *b fa* at the beginning, or which has a prescribed ♮ ♯ *mi*, so that vocables of all other keys above and below are adapted to *mi* on ♮ *mi*. I will subjoin examples of these hexachords immediately after the rules of solmization, for they clearly cannot be understood by young students at this time, when they have not yet learned the principles of solmization.

Why is the natural hexachord omitted here?

It is because we are given a far easier method of instruction by omitting it rather than considering it. For when its nomenclature is omitted a much clearer and more commodious division of all songs is effected by the presence or absence of *b* at the beginning. Moreover, by omitting it the art of solmization can be explained to youthful minds with far fewer and easier rules.

It does not matter that the natural hexachord has its own particular form in comparison with the other two, especially since it never occurs in this way without extending into the melodic range of the hard ♮ hexachord or the soft *b* hexachord, unless perhaps it does not go beyond a fifth. In such a case absolutely nothing prevents the name and rules of the hard ♮ hexachord from being applied to it.

How many important rules are included in a complete study of solmization?

There are seven, according to the seven letters *a b c d e f g* which the system contains. Although these letters are written first as capitals, then as small letters, and finally as doubled letters, because of different voice ranges, yet in so far as the art of solmization is concerned, whatever is sung on the central small letters applies equally to capital letters below and the doubled letters above. The same thing is stated by others, but more obscurely, when they say that octaves are considered the same.

Rules of Solmization

First rule: concerning *A re*, *a la mi re*, *aa la mi re*. If a hexachord with a soft *b* prefixed ascends beyond these keys, *mi* is sung on them; if soft *b* is not prefixed, *re* is sung on them. But if the hexachord descends more than a major third beyond them, *la* is always sung on them.

Comment: I say more than a major third, for if the hexachord descends only a major third or less *la* is not necessary, since the descent can be completed by *mi, re, ut*. The same thing should be understood concerning the lower range of other hexachords, namely that substitution of different vocables is not needed when a hexachord does not exceed *ut, re, mi, fa, sol, la*, its six vocables.

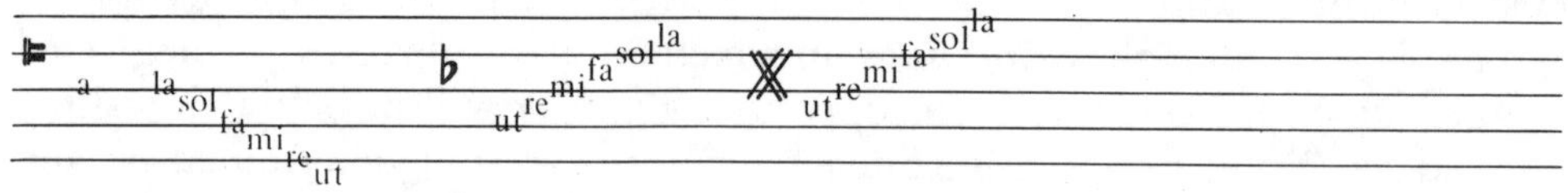

Second rule: concerning ♮ *fa*,[20] *b fa*, *bb fa*, ♮ *mi*. If the hexachord is soft *b*, *fa* is sung on them, but if it is hard ♮, *mi* is sung. Every hexachord that has a prefixed *b* is a soft *b* hexachord; every hexachord that does not have a prefixed *b* is a hard ♮ hexachord.

Third rule: concerning *C fa ut*, *c sol fa ut*, *cc sol fa*. If the hexachord ascends more than a major third above them, *ut* is always sung on them. If it descends a whole step with a prefixed *b*, *sol* is sung; if *b* is not prefixed *fa* is sung.

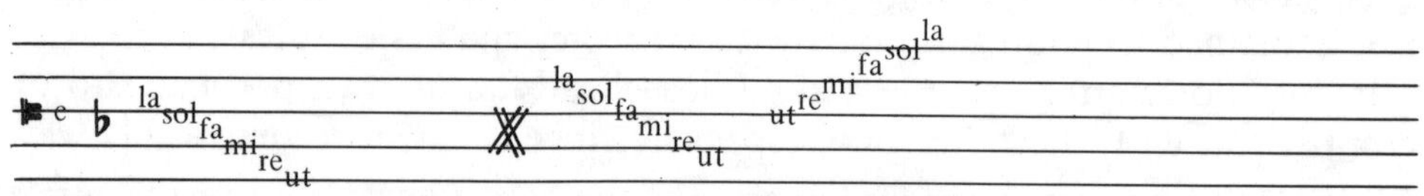

Fourth rule: concerning *D sol*, *d la sol re*, *dd la sol*. If the hexachord ascends more than a whole tone beyond them, *re* is always sung on them. If it does not ascend more than a whole tone but descends more than a whole tone and has a *b* prefixed, *la* is sung; if *b* is not prefixed sol is sung.[21]

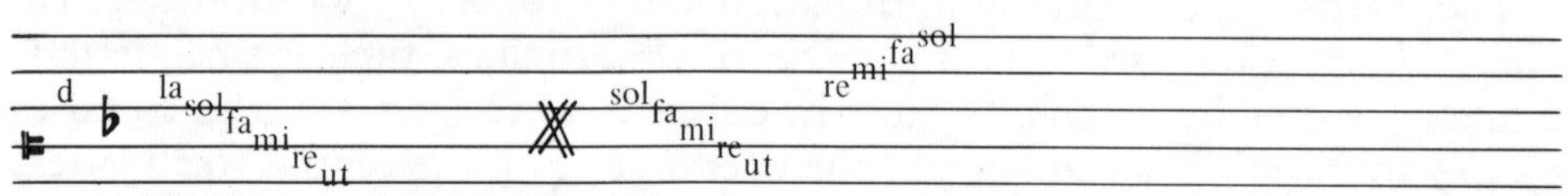

Fifth rule: concerning *E la mi*, *e la mi*, *ee la*. If the hexachord descends more than a major third below them *la* is always sung. If it descends less than a major third, or if it ascends, *mi* is always sung.

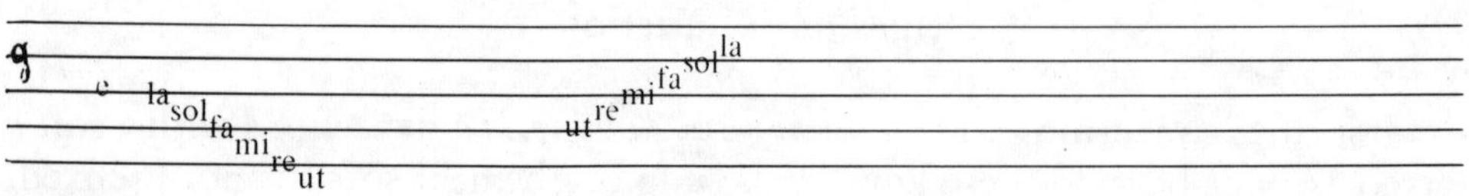

[20] The ♮ sign refers here to the third note of the gamut or *B*, which can be *mi* or *fa*.

[21] The clef sign in the example should be on the third line.

Sixth rule: concerning *F fa ut*, *f fa ut*.

Ut is sung when the hexachord ascends to *b fa* with a *b* prefixed; otherwise *fa* is always sung.

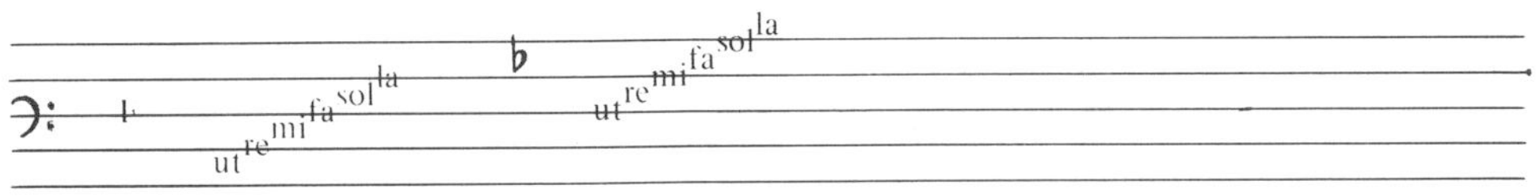

Seventh rule: concerning *Γ ut*, *G sol re ut*, *g sol re ut*. If the hexachord ascends more than a whole tone above them and *b* is prefixed, *re* is sung; if *b* is not prefixed *ut* is sung. If it does not ascend more than a whole tone, but rather descends, *sol* is always sung.

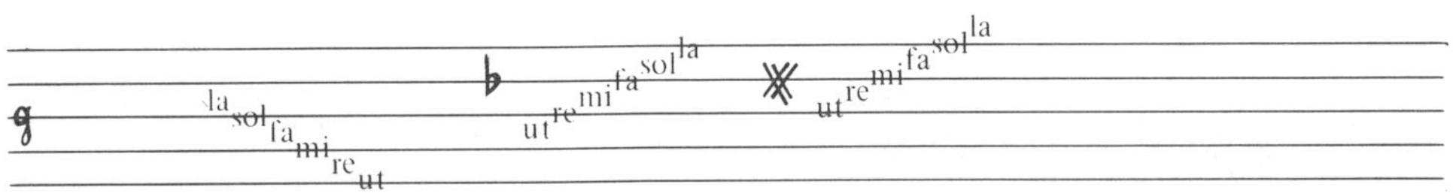

First additional comment: if *b fa* or ♮ *mi* is written at the beginning on a pitch other than its usual pitch, then the normal sequence of the entire system is disregarded, and the gamut of all other syllables and tones is applied according to the new pitch of *b fa* or ♮ *mi*.

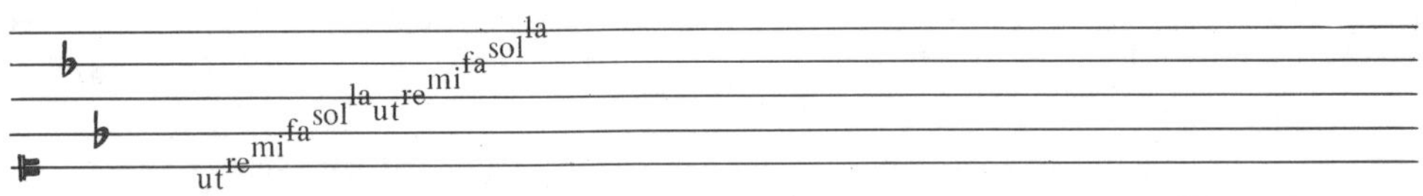

Second additional comment: if *b fa* is not prefixed at the beginning, but is inserted here and there in the middle of a song, it affects only the note that immediately follows it on the same line or space.

In the above rules the entire art of solmization is shown with clarity and brevity. By following them young boys can immediately recognize the vocables of all the notes after they have determined the characteristic key of the song, providing, as we taught earlier, that they have the entire system in their grasp and have memorized it. In this way, through the characteristic key one immediately sees what other characteristic keys lie above and below it. From these a particular scale of vocables based on *b fa* or ♮ *mi* is quickly revealed, so that just as any vocable of a scale may fall on any line or space, so also all succeeding notes are quickly and accurately recognized from this vocable. Characteristic keys were treated earlier.

The following illustrations show how, by means of a characteristic key alone, other keys and the vocable scale are recognized in any song; also, how mutations occur in ascending or descending beyond a hexachord.

Contents of the high system to which the *discantus* belongs.

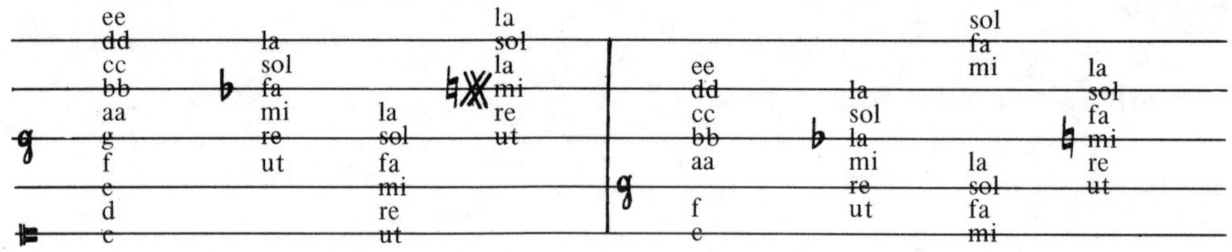

Contents of the middle system, common to the alto and tenor.

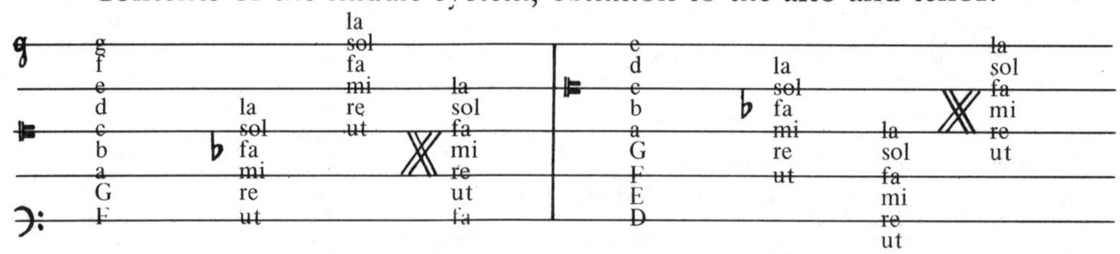

Contents of the low system to which the bass belongs.

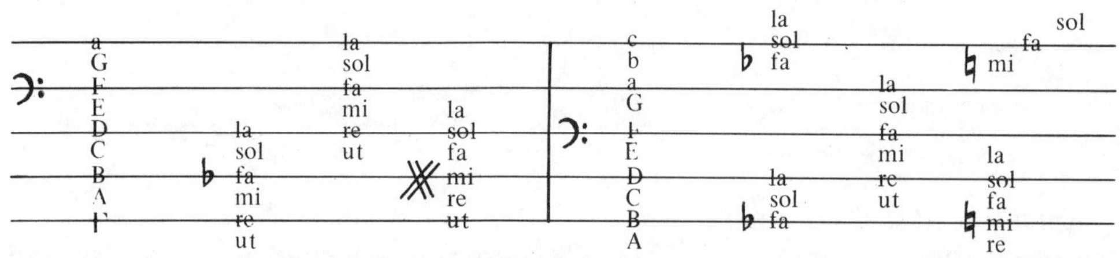

There follows as many examples of solmization as there are positions of characteristic keys in use, so that through these examples, studied carefully on hexachords, young students will then compare all similar ones to them, and will not hesitate to sol-fa (*solmifandum*), as we usually say, in the very same order and manner in all other similar cases. After they have done this they will be able to sing without the least hesitation any similar songs that are given to them.

First example in the high range, called *discantus*, on *g sol re ut* with hard ♮.

Ex. 2 An exercise in vocables by N.P.

Second example of the high range on *g sol re ut* with soft *b*.
Two-voice canon in which the second voice follows a measure later and a whole step higher.

Ex. 3 [*Pleni sunt* from *Missa Mater Patris* — Josquin des Prez]

Third example of the high range on *c* with soft *b*.

Ex. 4 *Fuga* of three voices, two in unison and a third a fifth below. Composer is unknown.

1 The discant *a* and *c* were originally semibreves and lacked the following rests.

Fourth example of the high range on *c* with hard ♮.

Two-voice canon, in which the second voice follows the first one measure later and a whole tone lower. Josquin.

Ex. 5 [*Benedictus* from *Missa Mater Patris* — Josquin des Prez]

First example in the middle range of the alto and tenor.

Ex. 6 Two-voice canon at the unison after one measure, by an unknown composer.

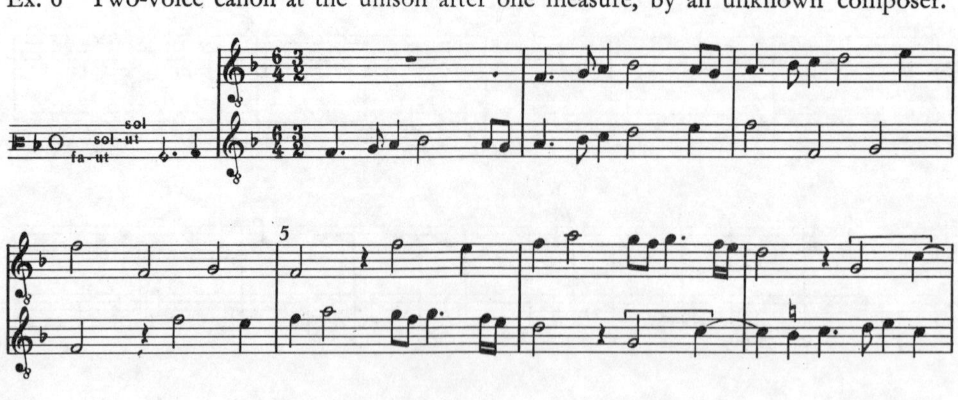

1 changed from *e* to *f*

Second example in the middle range of the alto and tenor, on *c sol fa ut* with hard ♮.

Ex. 7 Two-voice canon at the unison by an unknown composer.

1 This *ut sol* should be one step lower

Third example of the middle range on *c sol fa ut* with soft ♭.

Ex. 8 Three-voice canon at the unison.

1 Changed from *e* to *f*

1 Changed from *g* to *a*

Fourth example of the middle range using hard ♮.
Three-voice canon at the unison by an unknown composer.
Ex. 9 [*Sic unda impellitur unda*]

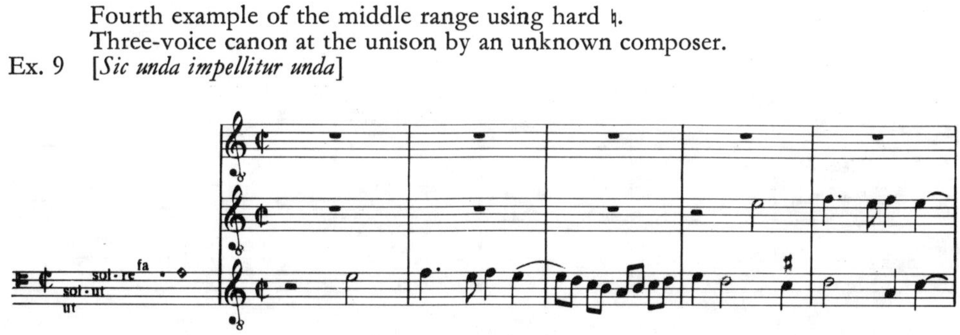

10
15
20
25
30
35
40

First example of the bass or lowest voice.
Two-voice canon at the unison. Iacobus Obrecht.
Ex. 10 [*Qui cum patre* from *Credo* of *Missa Salve diva parens*]

Second example of the lowest voice.
Two-voice canon at the unison. De Orto.
Ex. 11 [*Agnus Dei II* from *Missa j'ay pris amour* — Marbriano de Orto]

Third example of the lowest voice.
Two-voice canon at the fourth below [*recte* fifth above] by Josquin.
Ex. 12 [*Pleni sunt* from *Missa Hercules Dux Ferrariae*]

Example of *cantus fictus* using soft ♭ or hard ♮.

Three-voice canon at the fourth above after one measure. Okeghem.

Ex. 13 [*Prennez sur moi votre exemple amoureux* — Johannes Ockeghem]

CHAPTER 5

Tactus

Thus far I have discussed the scale, the constitution of keys, and the vocables to be applied in singing. These things are nothing but rules concerning the rise and fall of tones and voices. What now follows, however, will treat not the rise and fall of a tone but its length or shortness, for the quantity of a tone is twofold according to a consideration of its rise and fall or its lengthened and shortened value. Just as we have considered it through the lines and spaces of the scale, so now we will consider it through varied note shapes, in accordance with the longer or shorter duration of tones. While previously we measured it intervalically, now we measure it temporally. We recognize its temporal value by the *tactus*, so that it is necessary to consider the *tactus* before the notes.

What is *tactus*?

It is a movement or stroking motion of a finger fitting the value of all notes and rests into an equally divided temporal beat. The *tactus* therefore defines very accurately the temporal value of every note and rest. Moreover, nothing definite can be understood or taught about the length, perfection, imperfection, augmentation and diminution of notes unless previously the *tactus* has been definitely established.

Therefore,[22] we have established this kind of *tactus* here, in which one alternating and equidistant *tactus* corresponds to the time value of one semibreve under the signs *O*, *C*. All other larger or smaller notes should then be reckoned according to the equality of a *tactus* to a semibreve.

How many kinds of *tactus* are there?

Others teach that there are three kinds of *tactus*, which for a long time now have been accepted by the majority of singers. But if one views with greater perception the nature of this art, the nature of a proportion, and songs of the most excellent composers, he will be convinced in each instance that there is only one kind of *tactus* which can and should be adapted to proven songs of any kind. For if a *tactus* must be divided at all it does not make any difference if it moves faster or slower itself, but rather if it governs more or fewer notes.

When[23] older musicians desired a slower or faster song they showed this through longer or shorter note values and not through a faster or slower *tactus*, for no one can deny that diminution signs and proportions of *genus multiplex* came into music for this one reason alone.

Thus it is always necessary to divide note values in accordance with various signs of *modus*, *tempus*, *prolatio*, and *proportio*, and not the temporal value of the *tactus*. For in a song the same *tactus* makes one semibreve in *perfectus non diminutus* equal to two semibreves in *diminutus* or *proportio dupla*, to three semibreves in

[22] This paragraph does not appear in the 1537 edition.
[23] This paragraph is also lacking in the 1537 edition.

tripla, and to one and one-half semibreves in *sesquialtera*. We will defer a clearer presentation of this matter, in examples chosen from the best composers, until the last part of this book, since it is not appropriate to present them here, when young students still have not learned about *modi*, *prolationes*, *proportiones*, etc. Here it will be enough if young boys have learned that in dividing the values of notes and rests, the number of *tactus* equals the number of semibreves, in so far as they are not augmented or diminished. For the essential value of a semibreve equals a single *tactus*. But when semibreves are sometimes worth more or less according to various inscribed signs, that is not relative to their essence but to some accidental artifice.

CHAPTER 6

Notes

What are notes?

Notes are certain characters according to which tones and voices in songs are formed and directed.

What is required to properly recognize notes?

Two things: position and shape. The position of a note shows how far a tone should be raised or lowered in relation to what has been taught earlier about solmization. The shape of a note shows the length or shortness of a tone's duration. Related to these points is everything that will be taught afterwards concerning note values, dots, rests, *modus*, *tempus*, *prolatio*, augmentation and diminution.

How many types of notes are there?

Two: single notes and connected notes.

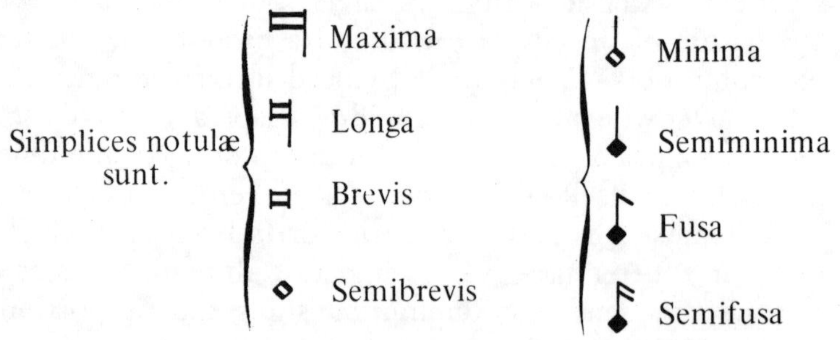

What is the value of single notes?

According to various *modi*, *tempora*, *prolationes*, and *proportiones*, they have a varied time value through their perfection or imperfection, augmentation or diminution, all of which will be treated in the second book on mensuration. But now it is enough to show very simply in a general form the value of each note as it is usually found.

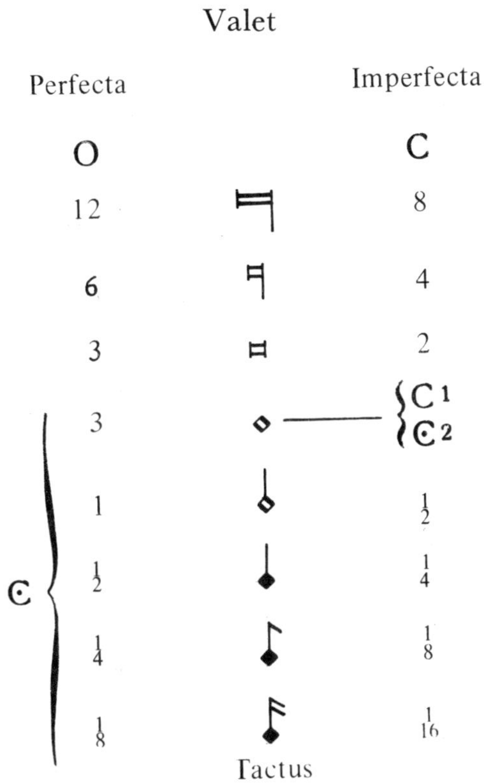

Which notes are connected?

They are those in which many simple notes are written together as if in a unit. Some think that their connection is the result of the application of a text, although in an extended series of notes the need for variety could also be given as a reason.

How are connected notes divided?

Into semibreves, breves, longs, and mixed notes.

How are semibreves written?

In two ways:

1. Two square note shapes connected at different levels, in which the first has a stem rising from its left side, as here: 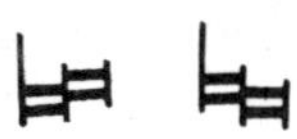
2. One note shape in the form of an oblique parallelogram, in which a stem also rises from the left, as here: 

Each of these note shapes has a natural value of two semibreves.

What are the shapes of connected breves?

They are also twofold:
1. Two square note shapes connected on
rising levels and lacking a stem as here: 
2. A single note shape in the shape of an oblique parallelogram,
in which a stem descends from the left, as here: 

Each note shape is equal to two breves. If they are perfect each one equals three *tactus*; if imperfect, each one equals two *tactus*. When the stem on the left ascends they are always semibreves; when it descends they are breves.

What are the shapes of connected longs?

They are also twofold:
1. Two square note shapes connected on descending
levels and lacking a stem as here: 

2. Several square note shapes connected on descending levels, in which
a stem ascends or descends from the right side of each, as here: 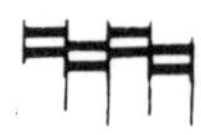

Stems on the right side belong only to longs and maximas.

What then are mixed ligatures?

They are connections of two, three, or more notes which have different time values. They occur when notes are added to the above single or connected notes. The following rules treat them very briefly.

First rule. Semibreve and breve ligatures are considered in exactly the same way as before when they prefix other notes. Example:

Second rule. All other accessory notes except the final note are breves unless a maxima is used. Examples:

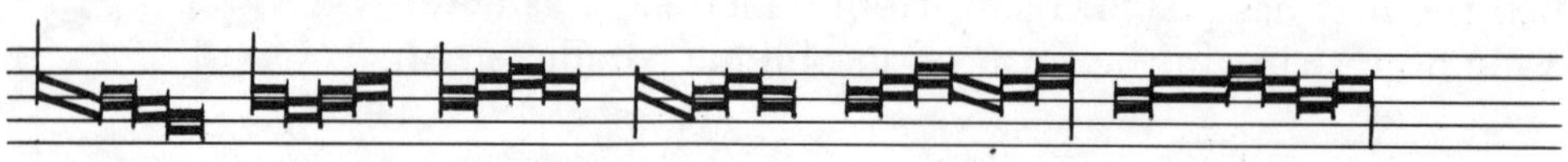

Third rule. All final stemless notes approached from below and all final oblique notes approached from above are breves. All final square notes with or without stems and approached from above are longs. Examples are the final notes of the above illustration.

Fourth rule. An initial square note without a stem and descending scalewise is a long. If it has a stem descending from the left, or if it ascends scalewise, it is a breve. Examples:

Fifth rule. If the initial note of an oblique ligature lacking a stem ascends or descends, the first note will be a long, the second a breve. Examples:

An example of every kind of note.
Ex. 14 *Fortuna* according to musical vocables, by Ludwig Senfl.

20
25
30
35
40
45

50
55
60
65
70
75

80
85
90
95
100
105

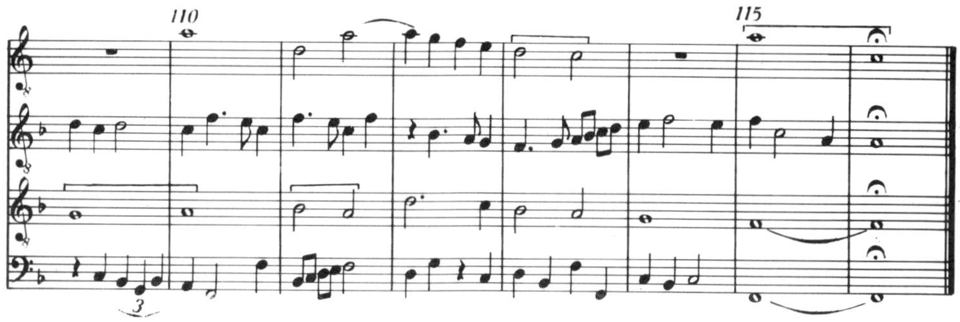

CHAPTER 7

Dots

How many kinds of dots are used in a song?

There are three kinds. One increases by one-half the value of a note it follows, and thus is called a *punctum additionis*. Another doubles the value of the second of two identical note values, and for this reason has acquired the name *punctum alterationis*. A third divides notes from other notes, and thus is called *punctum distinctionis* or *punctum divisionis*.

What is a *punctum additionis*?

It is the name usually given to a dot which is written directly after a note and which changes the note from a value of one to one and one-half; that is, it adds one-half more to a note's value than it had without the dot. A *punctum perfectionis* is also considered the same because it has the same result. Example:

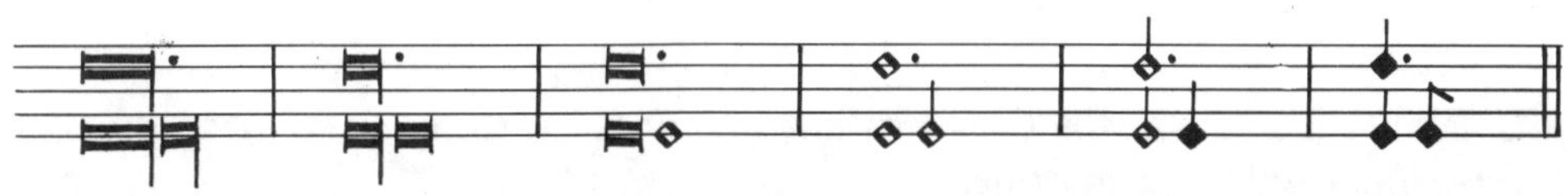

What is a *punctum divisionis*?

It is a sign written above the middle of a note group, either between two longs encompassed by two maximas in *modus maior perfectus*; or between two breves encompassed by two longs in *modus minor perfectus*; or between two semibreves encompassed by two breves in *tempus perfectum*; or between two minims encompassed by two semibreves in *prolatio maior*. The second book will treat *modus*, *tempus*, and *prolatio*. Example:

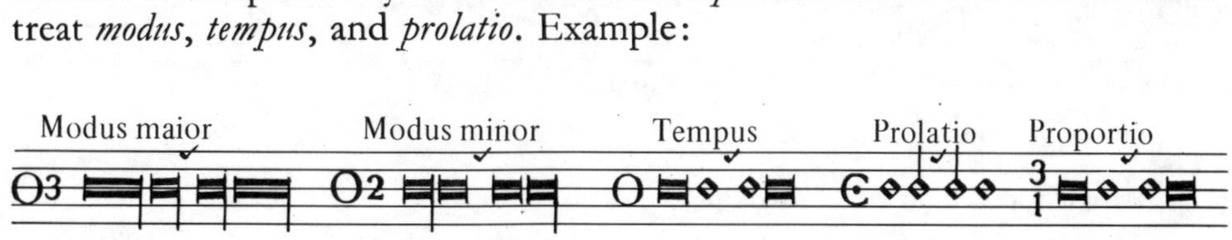

For what purpose is it placed above?

To give both larger outer notes a smaller middle note, so that both larger outer notes may attain a ternary perfection by the addition of a smaller middle note, since otherwise they are imperfect. For a *punctum divisionis* is applied only to a ternary division. Therefore, it is found only in songs which are inscribed at the beginning with a complete circle, or a number three, or with a dot of *prolatio maior*. All these will be discussed below.

What is a *punctum alterationis*?

It is a sign which is recognized in the same way as the other signs and which is also in the same note arrangement as the *punctum divisionis*. But it is actually different because it is either written obliquely above the first larger outer note, as at (a), or its part, as at (b), or an equivalent rest, as at (c). It doubles the value of the second smaller middle note following it. Thus it is called a *punctum alterationis*.

Sometimes[24] when a dot is missing alteration still occurs, which then must be understood from the ternary division. This happens when a semibreve ligature in *tempus perfectum* is encompassed by two breves, even if no *punctus divisionis* is written above, for the last note of the ligature is doubled and the first breve retains its perfection, as at (d). Examples:

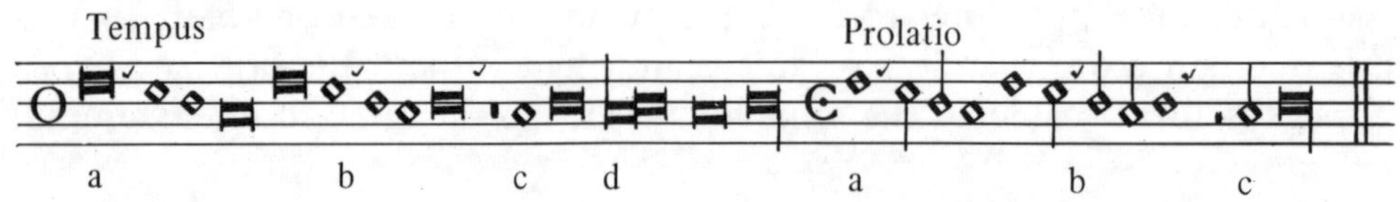

But what if a *punctum divisionis* or *alterationis* is written above many smaller notes encompassed by larger ones?

In examples of this kind the ternary division must be followed without fail. If it is carefully observed, even if dots are lacking, it shows very clearly not only into which ternary group every note fits, but also which notes should be doubled or altered, as they say, because a ternary grouping is lacking.

[24] This paragraph is lacking in the 1537 edition.

CHAPTER 8

Rests

What is a rest in music?

It is a line of definite length which is drawn through staff lines and which shows how much of the *tactus* and time must pass in silence.

How many kinds of rests are there?

There are as many kinds as there are notes. Each note has its own rest, so that a rest should have the same value as its note in the same song.

How are rests recognized?

By the varied number of lines. If three lines extend through three complete spaces and touch four staff lines they are called rests of *modus maior* or of a perfect maxima, as at (a). But if two lines, they are rests of an imperfect maxima, as at (b).

Maxima

Perfecta Imperfecta

a b

If one such line or many unequally placed lines touch four staff lines the rests belong to *modus minor perfectus* or a perfect long, as at (c).

Longa perfecta

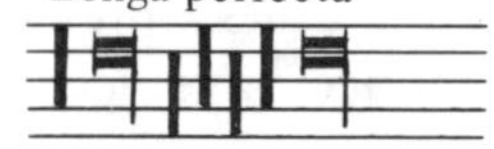

c

A line reaching the third staff line is an imperfect long rest, as at (d).

Longa imperfecta

d

A line reaching the next staff line is a breve rest, as at (e).

Brevis

e

A line hanging from a staff line to the middle of the space below is called a semibreve rest, as at (f). Two of these rests hanging from the same line indicate *tempus perfectum*, as at (g).

Semibrevis

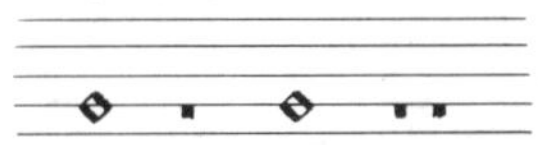

f g

A line which rises from a staff line to the middle of the space above is called a minim rest or a *suspirium*, as at (h). If it is written twice in the same space it indicates *prolatio perfecta*, as at (i).

Minima

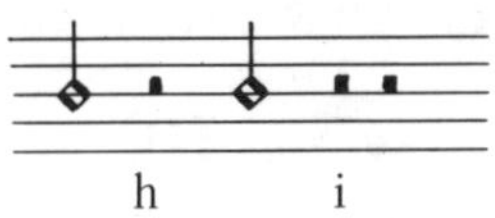

h i

A line which also rises from a staff line but with a hook extending to the right at the tip, is a semiminim rest, as at (k).

Semiminima

k

If the rest has two hooks it is a *fusa*, as at (l). If it has three hooks it is a *semifusa*, as at (m).

Fusa Semifusa

l m

The preceding rests are always equal in value to the notes whose names they bear, but are free from any alteration or imperfection and retain the value of a perfect time signature when it applies. Besides these rests certain other signs are added, which, although they are more truly lesser signs of organization and unrelated to note values, are still studied thoroughly.

A rainbow-shaped semicircle with an enclosed dot, when placed above a note, indicates a general pause in all voices, as 𝄐. When two semicircles are joined back to back at the circumference of their sides, as :)(:, they show as many repetitions of the beginning as dots are inscribed within each curved line.

The preceding instruction is sufficient now for the first book. Since these teachings have been treated very simply they might have been appropriately called *musica simplex* or *musica choralis*, especially since the relation of scale to solmization is clearly the same in each. Nothing further about *musica choralis* is missing here, except that I chose to defer a description of the Tones until the last part of the second book, since young students cannot recognize them well at all unless previously they have learned to sing correctly and through long practice have accustomed their ears in some degree to recognizing melodies.

BOOK 2

Music, that is, the Art of Singing

PREFACE

Thus far I have taken pains to proceed in a way similar to that of good painters with their pupils. For when they give instruction in painting they do not use brushes and mixtures of colors before they have accustomed their pupils for some time to making pencil sketches. In the same way I also did not want to teach anything about various note values in diverse signs until young students had learned thoroughly the most simple principles of the scale, keys, notes, *tactus*, rests and dots.

But since these things have been taught so carefully in the first book that they can be understood and completely mastered by anyone who does not lack at least some intelligence, it is now possible to proceed with that part of music which appears to be most difficult because of the fact that either color or some other prescribed signs repeatedly change the value of almost all notes, rests and dots. This mutation or change of note values can be described here under the name mensuration, because through it we measure the value of any note under any sign. Under this appropriate term, mensuration, the accidental values of notes, so to speak, could be added to the above statement about notes, unless through a clearer understanding of this matter I am able to gather together so many mensural values in songs and so many enormous intricacies of signs and canonic prescripts into a definite rule, especially since I have frequently heard not only tyros but also distinguished musicians not in actual contention but still expressing complete doubt concerning the comparative meaning of various signs.

This is not strange, since there is also not sufficient agreement about the subject among composers (*componistae*), as they are usually called. Since many of them, disregarding the true observance of art, idly concoct enigmas rather than songs, just as if the use of signs did not follow certain laws and could be applied at will, confusion has resulted in all respects. But if we clearly demonstrate through the most esteemed musicians, as Josquinus, Brymelus, Obertus, Isaacus, and similar men, that everything we have taught here on the subject is true, why will we not appear worthy of trust?

CHAPTER 1

Mensuration

What is mensuration?

It is a certain passage of time divided equally by a *tactus*. In it notes and rests of all songs are sung according to the temporal meaning of a sign.

How many kinds of mensuration are there?

Six: *prolatio*, *tempus*, *modi*, *proportio*, augmentation and diminution. Through them the value of notes is continually changed in songs, so that they are sung as perfect, imperfect, augmented or diminished note values. *Prolatio* is applied in semibreves, *tempus* in breves, *modus* in longs and maximas. Proportions, augmentation and diminution can be applied in all of them.

What does it mean if notes are perfect?

It means that they are reckoned in threes, so that each larger note contains the next smaller note three times. In this way a maxima equals three longs, a long three breves, a breve three semibreves and a semibreve three minims.

By how many kinds of signs is perfection recognized?

By two kinds. Some are seen at the beginning of songs and others occur in the middle. Initial signs are found in older songs, as perfect long rests, a complete circle with or without numbers and a dot written within a circle. Middle signs are three blackened notes of the same kind, two semibreve rests hanging from the same line, as ┬┬, or two minim rests rising from the same line, as ┴┴.

Finally, anywhere young students see dots of division or alteration written above notes they will be certain of a perfection at that place.

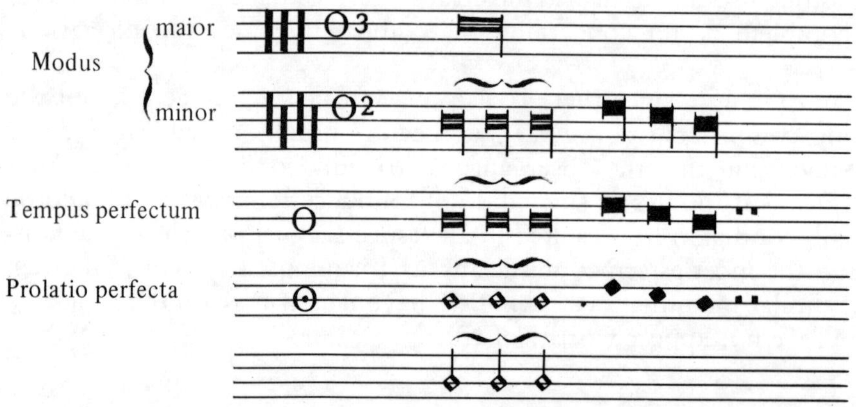

What does it mean if notes are imperfect?

It means that they are reckoned in twos, so that a larger note contains the next smaller note twice. In this way a maxima equals two longs, a long two breves, a breve two semibreves and a semibreve two minims.

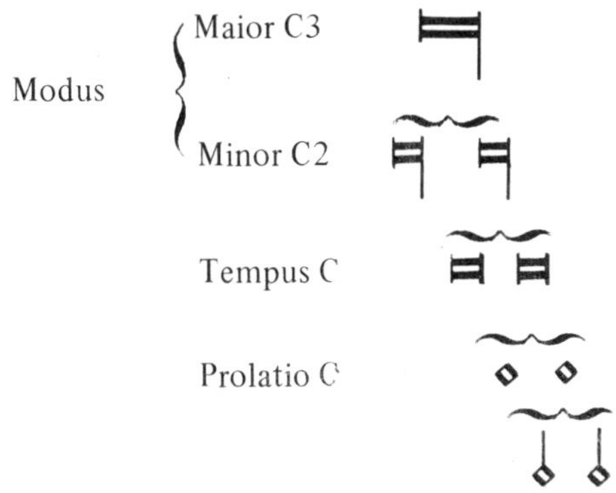

By what signs is imperfection recognized?

By the semicircles C, ¢, C2, and C without a dot. Since all of these signs apply to certain notes, I will give three rules which elucidate the subject very clearly.

First rule: in O, C, ɸ, ¢, a complete circle without numbers or dots indicates *tempus perfectum* or the perfection of breves; a half circle indicates *tempus imperfectum* or imperfection of breves.

Second rule: if number two or three is added after a circle, as O3, C3, O2, C2, the circle properly pertains to *modi*. A circle with number three applies to maximas and a circle with number two applies to longs. But the three shows *tempus perfectum* and the two *tempus imperfectum*.

Third rule: when dots are inscribed in circles or semicircles, as ⊙, C, ɸ, ¢, they always refer to *prolatio* or *semibreves*. But the circles still follow the first two rules, so that if a number is added the circle will refer to *modi*, and if not, to *tempus*.

Here[25] young students should be warned that the rules prescribed above on signs agree more with songs of newer composers than with those of older musicians. The latter showed *modus maior perfectus* by three perfect long rests equally placed at the beginning, and *modus maior imperfectus* by two. If they are written at the beginning in front of a sign of *tempus*, they are only signs and are not counted as rests in singing. If they are placed after a sign of *tempus* they are counted, as here:

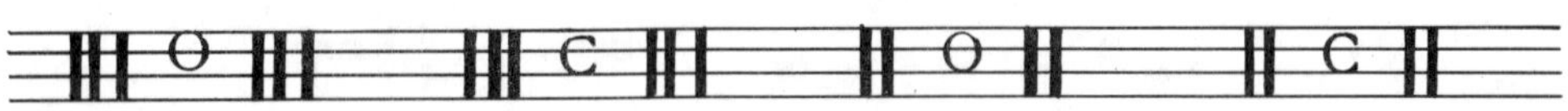

Modus maior perfectus cum tempore perfecto	Modus maior perfectus cum tempore imperfecto	Modus maior imperfectus cum tempore perfecto	Modus maior imperfectus cum tempore imperfecto

Older musicians showed *modus minor perfectus* by one perfect long rest, also by two that sometimes were equally placed, or by more that were unequally placed. Here are examples:

[25] The next three paragraphs are lacking in the 1537 edition.

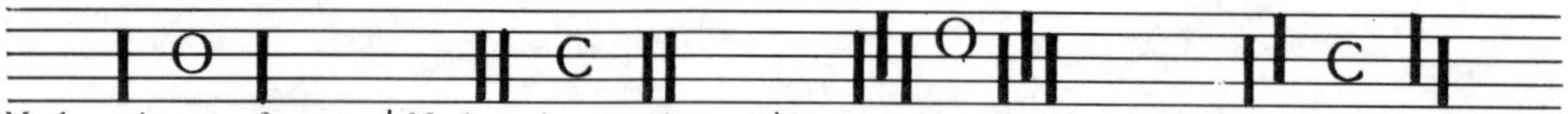

Modus minor perfectus cum tempore perfecto	Modus minor perfectus cum tempore imperfecto	Modus minor perfectus cum tempore perfecto	Modus minor perfectus cum tempore imperfecto

They wanted *modus minor imperfectus* to be understood when no perfect long rests were placed at the beginning, or when a group of three blackened longs was not found in a song. But contrary to the first rule, with a circle and number two, O2, they indicated not *modus* but *tempus* with *proportio dupla.* A circle alone showed *tempus*, not *modus* — *tempus perfectum* with a complete circle, *tempus imperfectum* with a half circle. If they wrote a double circle, as ⦾, the outer circle showed *modus*, the inner *tempus*. A complete circle in either indicated perfection, a half circle imperfection, as Ͼ, ⦾, Ͼ. Wherever they wrote a number after a circle they meant not *tempus* but proportions, number three for *proportio tripla* and number two for *proportio dupla.*

Now, before beginning the treatment of individual kinds of mensuration, it seems necessary to discuss the kind of imperfection which occurs most frequently in perfect mensurations. Since it is common to *prolatio*, *tempus*, and both *modi*, and since it is found in perfect mensurations, one may term it an imperfection of perfection.

What is imperfection of perfection?

It occurs when some notes that should be perfect in their own right are counted as binary because of certain accidental reasons. The things that are taught about perfect notes (semibreves in *prolatio*, breves in *tempus*, longs and maximas in both *modi*) do not depend as much on any first note as on other following notes and rests. Thus it happens that a preceding note in perfect mensuration loses its perfection through succeeding notes or rests, that is, it must be considered as binary and not ternary. The following rules are useful for a clearer perception and understanding of imperfection and the ways in which it occurs.

First rule: in perfection, every perfect note in a perfect mensuration retains its perfection when the note or rest immediately following is the same value, as (a), or larger, as (b).

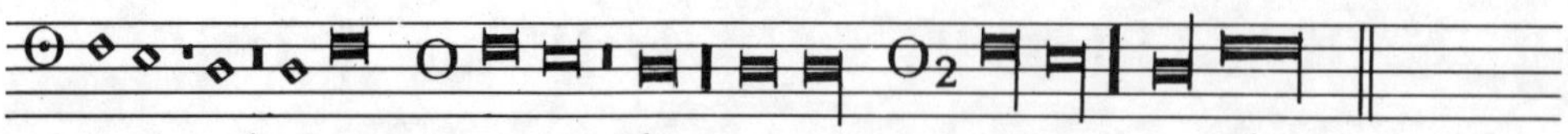

a b a b a b

Second rule: in imperfection of perfection, if a note in a perfect mensuration is blackened, as (a), or is followed by a smaller note, as (b), or rest, as (c), it is considered imperfect or binary.

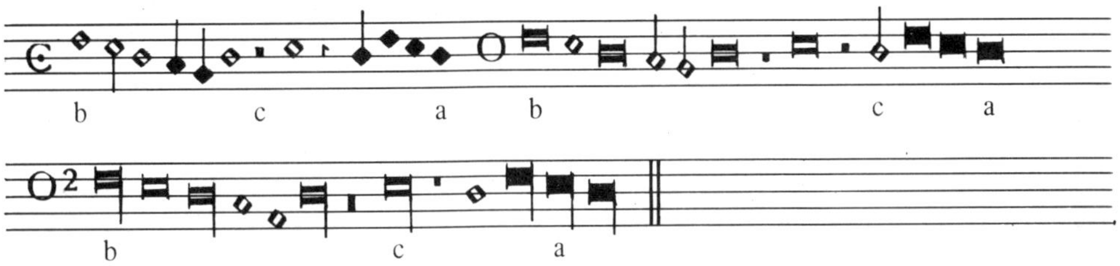

Third rule: in exception to the second rule, when a preceding larger note in a perfect mensuration is followed by a smaller note or rest, it is not imperfected when a *punctum alterationis* is applied, as (a), or a *punctum additionis*, as (b). or if some smaller notes or rests are interposed which in themselves form a ternary perfection without regard for the larger outer notes, as (c).

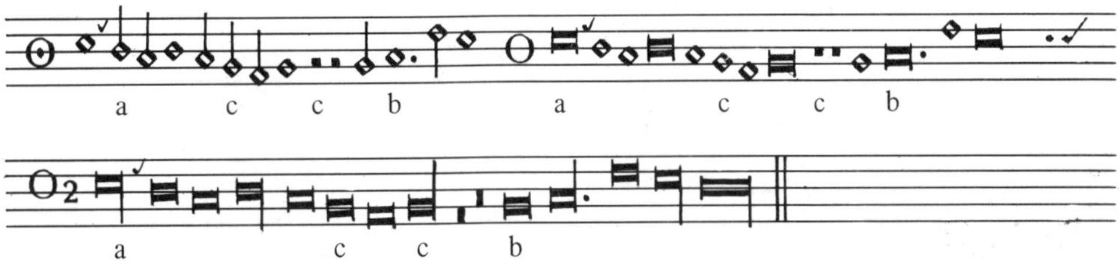

Fourth rule: in blackening notes, a third part of notes is removed in perfect mensuration, as (a), and a fourth part of notes in imperfect mensuration, as (b). Thus a blackened breve in perfect mensuration equals only two semibreves, as (a), and in imperfect mensuration it equals a semibreve and a minim, as (b). In the same way a blackened semibreve in *prolatio maior* equals only two minims, as (a), and in *prolatio minor* it equals a minim and a semiminim, as (b).

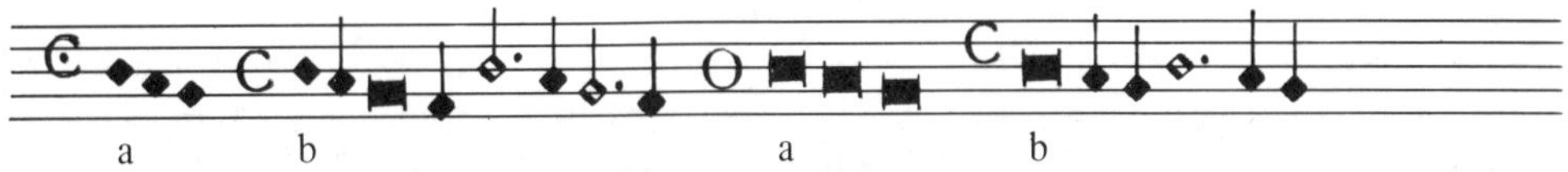

If many notes are blackened the blackening rather frequently causes a *hemiolia* proportion, and sometimes *proportio dupla*. Each will be studied later with its own examples.

First annotation: on imperfection which some call partial. If one semibreve note or rest follows a long in *tempus perfectum*, imperfection is ascribed not to the long but to the second of the two breves it contains. And if a minim immediately follows a breve in *prolatio maior*, imperfection is ascribed not to the breve but to the second of the two semibreves it contains. For truly careful observation of the ternary division always teaches that just as every perfection must be reckoned according to it, so also any imperfection can easily be found without fail.

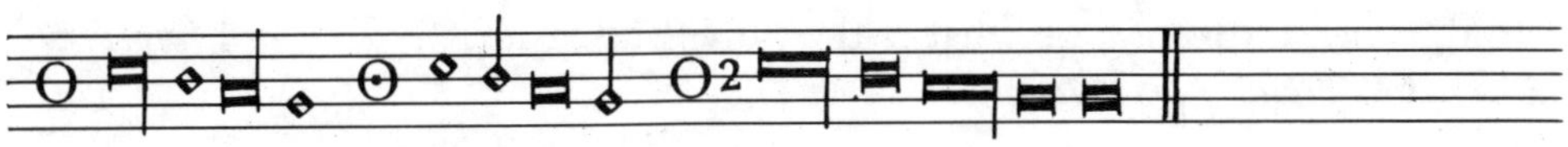

Second annotation: now and then a larger note in perfect mensuration is not imperfected by a following note but by the closest preceding smaller note, and even by a preceding note much farther removed. No more definite rule concerning this imperfection or transference of a note value can be given than that the *punctum divisionis* and the ternary division of perfection must be carefully observed. From these two it is easy to discover which of the smaller notes should be considered and how much of the larger note should be sung.

Example of Brumelius [from *Missa Victimae paschali*], in which the fifth long is imperfected.

Example of Josquinus from [Kyrie II of *Missa*] *L'homme armé sexti toni*, in which the second semibreve is transferred to imperfect the last breve.

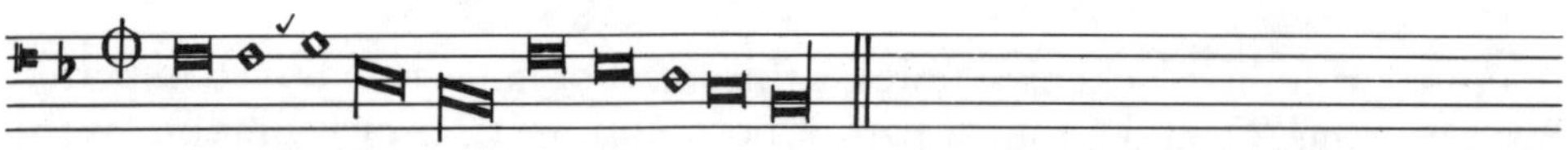

Now that this preliminary material is completed I will treat each kind of mensuration individually. While hoping to keep peace with other musicians in the following discussion, I should now like to change the usual order of presentation and to discuss first *prolatio*, and then in turn *tempus*, *modi*, proportions, augmentation, and finally diminution.

The usage of mensurations also demands that the value of semibreves should be established before proceeding to longs and maximas. What is easier and more self evident than that the latter be treated after the simpler notes? Certainly breves, longs and maximas are composed of simple semibreves, and so the value of each of them cannot be correctly described other than through the value of semibreves, undoubtedly because semibreves are always found in breves, longs, and maximas, while the latter are never found in semibreves.

CHAPTER 2

Prolatio

What is *prolatio*?

It is a mensuration in which the value of a semibreve is defined. It is twofold, *maior* and *minor*, or what is the same but easier, *perfecta* and *imperfecta*.

What is *prolatio perfecta*?

It is a mensuration in which a semibreve in a song equals three minims, and each minim receives one *tactus*. This is seen in a song when an encircled dot in one voice part is opposed to various undotted signs in other voices, although there are some who contend that an encircled dot in opposition to the undotted signs of other voice parts indicates augmentation and not *prolatio maior*. They believe that in *prolatio maior* three minims or one and one-half semibreves should be sung in each proportionate *tactus*, while in augmentation a complete *tactus* should be sung to each minim.

But I still do not see what can be cited from an established art to justify such an assertion. Of course it is true that *prolatio perfecta* very correctly can be called augmentation when it is opposed to *prolatio imperfecta*. It is also true that *prolatio perfecta*, as well as *tempus perfectum*, can be made into *proportio tripla*, or rather *sesquialtera*, and has been done so by many. But to do this according to diverse signs rather than according to the same kind of sign is really not acceptable to me.

Two absurdities arising from such an opinion can be cited. First, concerning the invention of many kinds of *tactus*, it is clearly not needed at all, since it is not only convenient but also necessary for true art that one and the same *tactus* be used in songs of all kinds. Second, it must be acknowledged of necessity that *prolatio maior* is worth less than *minor* if in *maior* each minim is not sung to a complete *tactus*, but a group of three minims is sung to a proportionate *tactus*. In this way three minims in *prolatio maior* are worth no more than two minims in *minor*, inasmuch as such a proportional *tactus*, which they teach without regard for the art, undoubtedly demands *proportio tripla* in this case. I certainly maintain concerning *prolatio maior integra*, ⊙ C·, *prolatio maior diminuta*, ⦶, ₵, as well as *prolatio maior* proportionata $⦶^3_2$, $₵^3_2$, that just as there is a difference between their signs so also is there a difference between their note values. Namely, in *prolatio maior integra* a perfect semibreve is worth three *tactus*, an imperfect semibreve two, and a minim one. But in *diminuta* one half of this value is sung, and in *proportionata* only a third. An example will show this a little later.

By what signs is *prolatio perfecta* recognized?

By dots placed in the middle of circles or semicircles, as ⊙, C·. Sometimes it is also shown without dots by three blackened semibreves or two minim rests rising uniformly from the same staff line, as 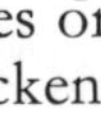. Therefore when young students see any of these signs in a song they shall know that it is in *prolatio maior* and that they should sing a perfect semibreve with three *tactus* and a minim with one *tactus*; also that in larger notes and rests they should augment the value of smaller notes and rests as many times as they are contained in the larger notes. Young boys should also remember here the rules we set down earlier on imperfection of perfect notes and should follow them in examining all notes in perfect time signatures, so that they do not accidentally keep them perfect in one case and make them imperfect in another.

What is *prolatio imperfecta*?

It is a mensuration in which one semibreve, equal to two minims, receives one *tactus*. It is to the value of a semibreve, as if to a fixed goal, that every sign of *modi*, *tempus*, proportion, augmentation and diminution should be referred and judged.

By what signs is *prolatio imperfecta* recognized?

It occurs only if no dot is written in a circle, for the presence of a dot indicates *prolatio maior*, and its absence *prolatio minor*.

Examples of everything that practice needs to know about *prolatio maior*.

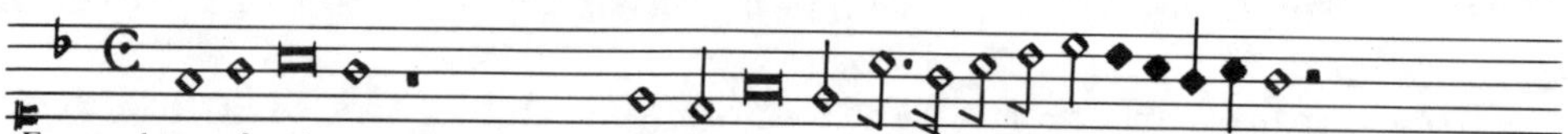

Exempla perfectionis Exempla imperfectionis

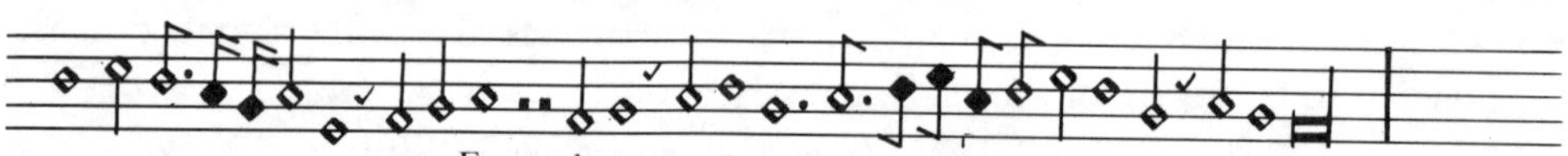

Exempla exceptionum

How many kinds of prolation are there?[26]

Three: *integra*, *diminuta*, *proportionata*. In *prolatio integra* a minim is worth one *tactus*, an imperfect semibreve is worth two, and a perfect semibreve is worth three, under the signs ⊙ , C· .

In *prolatio diminuta* two minims or one imperfect semibreve are worth one *tactus* and a perfect semibreve is worth one and one-half *tactus*, under the signs Φ, ₵.

In *prolatio proportionata*, through *sesquialtera* three minims or a perfect semibreve are worth one *tactus* under the signs Φ$\frac{3}{2}$, ₵$\frac{3}{2}$.[27]

Example of *prolatio maior integra*, *diminuta*, and *proportionata*.

Ex. 15 [Kyrie II from *Missa Quant j'ay au cueur* — Heinrich Isaac]

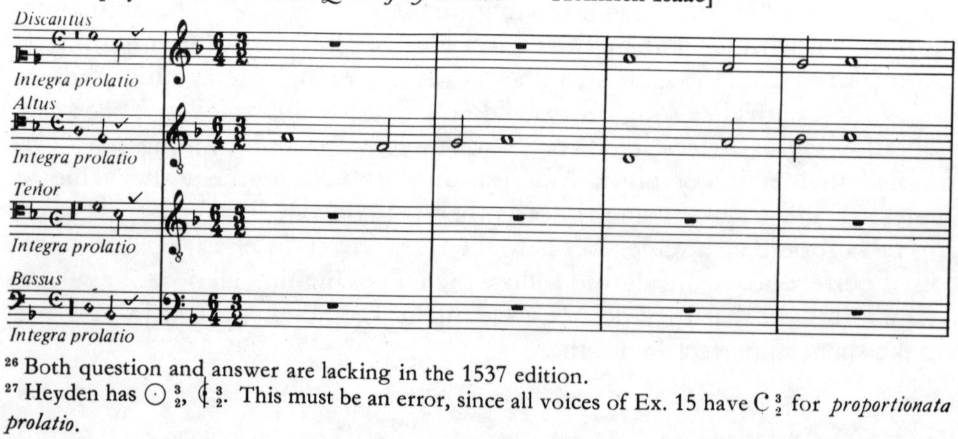

[26] Both question and answer are lacking in the 1537 edition.

[27] Heyden has ⊙$\frac{3}{2}$, ₵$\frac{3}{2}$. This must be an error, since all voices of Ex. 15 have C$\frac{3}{2}$ for *proportionata prolatio*.

Now follows another example or *prolatio perfecta* from *Missa Prolationum* by Iohannes Okeghem, in which perfect notes in *prolatio maior* are imperfected by blackening, and then all white and black notes in this mensuration are placed in diminution or *prolatio dupla*. This was done in *integra* mensurations, contrary to art and the practice of others. But we think that this probably happened through an error of copyists, since the mensuration signs do not have the proper intersecting lines which the concordance and measurement of the composition necessarily demands.

Ex. 16 [*Kyrie I* from *Missa Prolationum* — Johannes Ockeghem]

In *prolatio perfecta* young students sometimes also find half-blackened breves which they should resolve in this way: since such a breve contains two semibreve parts in *tempus imperfectum*, the first white semibreve part is perfect because of the dot of prolation and is worth three *tactus*, but the second blackened semibreve part is imperfected by its color and is worth only two *tactus*. Such is the case if the mensuration signs are *integra*. But if they are *diminuta* through a transverse line, as ₵, or a reverse semicircle, as Ɔ, or an added *proportio dupla*, as ₵ $\frac{2}{1}$, then the notes keep only one half of their prescribed value. The following example is taken from *Missa Bon temps* by Brumelius.

Another example follows [from *Missa Paschalis*] by Henricus Isaac.

Ex. 17 *Sanctus*

CHAPTER 3

Mensuration of tempus

What is mensuration of *tempus*?

It is a mensuration in which the value of a breve is defined according to how many or how few semibreves or *tactus* it includes.

How many kinds of *tempus* are there?

Two: perfect and imperfect. *Tempus* is perfect when a breve equals three semibreves.

By what mensuration signs is it recognized?

By a complete circle without numbers, as O, or circles with number three added, as O3, C3. Perfection is also generally indicated by other disguised signs, as three blackened breves or two semibreve rests hanging from the same staff line. Young students can also recognize perfection if a song has a *punctum divisionis* or *alterationis*, because these dots are used only to measure a ternary perfection.

What is *tempus imperfectum*?

It shows that a breve equals two semibreves.

By what mensuration signs is it recognized?

By a half circle without numbers, as C, or by number two added to circles, as O2, C2. The latter are used by more recent composers.

The following examples show everything necessary to know about perfect and imperfect breves.

Exempla perfectionis Exempla imperfectionis

Exempla exceptionum

How many kinds of *tempus* are there?

Three: *integrum*, *diminutum*, *proportionatum*. In *tempus integrum* a semibreve is worth one *tactus*, an imperfect breve is worth two *tactus*, and a perfect breve is worth three *tactus* under the signs O, C.

In *tempus diminutum* a semibreve is worth one-half of a *tactus*, an imperfect breve is worth a complete *tactus*, and a perfect breve is worth one and one-half *tactus* under the signs ⦶, ₵.

In *tempus proportionatum* two, three, four or more semibreves are worth one *tactus* under the proportions $\frac{2}{1}$, $\frac{3}{1}$, $\frac{4}{1}$, $\frac{3}{2}$.

Example of *tempus perfectum integrum*, *diminutum* and *proportionatum*.
Ex. 18 [*Kyrie II* from *Missa Quant j'ay au cueur* — Heinrich Isaac]

Since it appears to young boys that songs full of many *fusae* and thorny *suspiria* rests are generally very difficult, I decided to add here a difficult example and then resolve it from *integra* perfection into *diminuta* imperfection, so that anyone may see it is not so much through any difficulty as through its unusual appearance that such intricate songs are usually sung less expeditiously. If one looks carefully at the *resolutio* given for the following example, he will find nothing that is not very common and easy. On the contrary, everything in it agrees exactly in all respects with *integra* perfection, so that if you listen from a distance to both versions being sung you cannot determine whether *integra perfectio* or *diminuta resolutio* is sung.

Every *diminuta resolutio* will be sung correctly if it is sung as *dupla proportio*, just as all songs with the sign ₵ should be sung. We will discuss this later.

Through the following example young students can become practised in all such intricate songs, namely, by resolving *integra* perfection into imperfect diminution and then singing the resolution in *proportio dupla*.

Ex. 19 *Kyrie I* from [*Missa*] *Malheur me bat* — A. Agricola

CHAPTER 4

Mensuration of modus

What is mensuration of modus?

It is a mensuration which prescribes definite values for longs and maximas. *Modus* is twofold, *minor* and *maior*, because it controls two different notes, longs and maximas.

What is *modus minor*?

It is a mensuration which gives a perfect or imperfect value to a long. In *modus minor perfectus* a long is worth three breves, in *imperfectus* two breves.

By what signs are they recognized?

A complete circle followed by number two, as O2, is a sign of perfection. A half circle with number two, as C2, is a sign of imperfection. Older musicians omitted number two and indicated *modus minor perfectus* by perfect long rests or three blackened longs.[28]

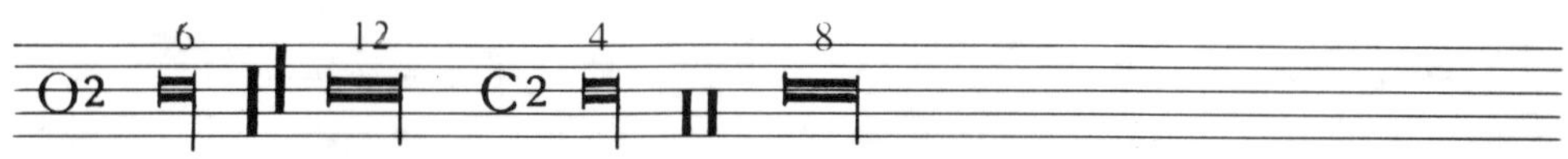

The following examples show everything necessary to know about perfect and imperfect longs.

[28] The *tactus* numbers of the longs and maximas in this example of O2 and C2 are halved in the later *tactus* tables, in which O2 and C2 are *semper diminuta*.

Perhaps[29] it would be pertinent to mention here this peculiarity of signsof *modi*: when their mensuration signs are written at the beginning they are hardly ever cancelled by smaller mensuration signs which follow, but continue in effect to the end in relation to their own notes, that is, to longs and maximas. But while these signs retain their value with other smaller succeeding signs, they have an effect on notes which are subject to them. Thus in the Ghiselin examples subjoined a little later one sees that several times the *tempus* mensuration is changed by changing the kind of circle used, but *modus* remains unchanged.

A similar case occurs later in the bass of the example of the third Tone,[30] in which the meaning of *modus minor perfectus*, together with its diminution, extends through all other smaller signs up to the last but imperfect sign of this *modus*. But in considering this sign of *modus minor*, O2, singers must be certain to weigh carefully whether it is written at the beginning in accordance with older or newer usage, for it is most important whether *tempus* or *modus* is meant by the circle, and whether *proportio dupla* or *tempus imperfectum* is meant by the number two. We will distinguish more exactly between these possibilities later in a table of resolutions.

Simultaneous example of *prolatio*, *tempus* and *modus minor*.

Ex. 20 [*Agnus Dei I* from *Missa ut re mi fa sol la* — Antoine Brumel]

[29] This paragraph and the next are not found in the 1537 edition.

[30] Ex. 49.

What is *modus maior*?

It is a mensuration which determines the length of time a maxima should be sung, and gives three longs to a perfect maxima, two to an imperfect maxima. A complete circle with number three, O3, indicates perfection, and a half circle with number three, C3, indicates imperfection.

But[31] these signs are current among more recent musicians, for, as we have already mentioned, older musicians were accustomed to show *modus maior perfectus* with three long rests placed on the same staff lines, and *modus maior imperfectus* with two long rests, just as one sees here in *Missa Gratieusa* of Iohannes Ghiselin. We decided to present two examples of this mensuration.

An example by Ghiselin, in which three perfect long rests show *modus maior perfectus*, a complete circle shows *tempus perfectum*, and number two shows *proportio dupla*.

[31] This paragraph is lacking in the 1537 edition.

An example in which two perfect long rests show *modus maior imperfectus*, a complete circle shows *tempus perfectum*, a half circle shows *tempus imperfectum*, a dot shows *prolatio perfecta*, and number two shows *proportio dupla*.
[*Credo* from *Missa Gratieusa*]

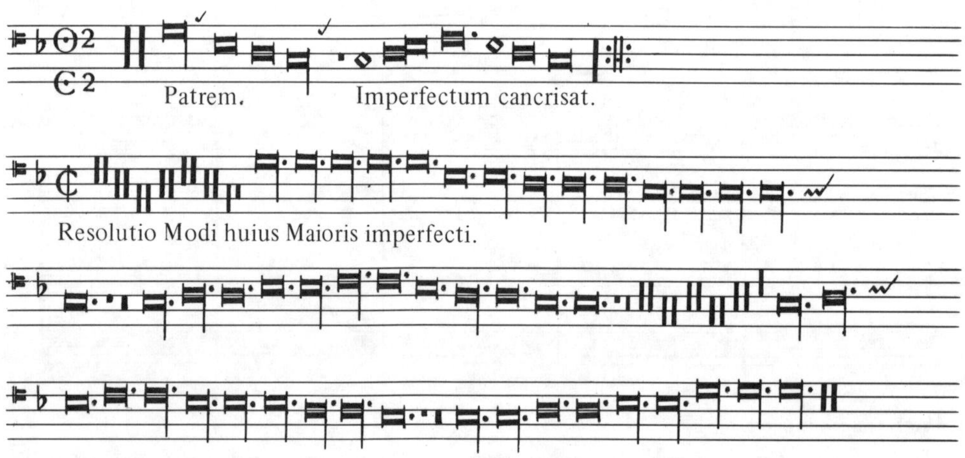

But here it is obvious, unless I am mistaken, that the value of breves, longs, and maximas cannot really be determined unless previously the value of *prolationes* has been defined. For each modus always contains *tempus* and *tempus* is never without either *prolatio*. Thus *prolatio* is common to *modus* and *tempus*, since it is *maior* when written in a circle, and *minor* when not written. So, if *prolatio maior* is added to *tempus* or *modi* by a dot, the value of larger notes will be completely different than if a dot were lacking, since through the dot each semibreve in larger notes is tripled in value.

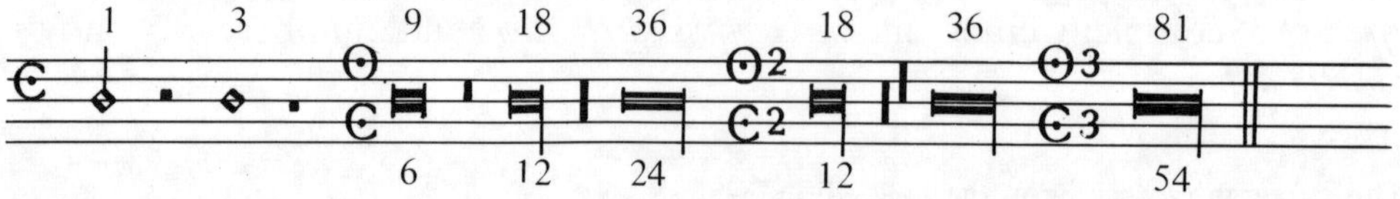

But if *prolatio* is *minor* and lacks a dot, each larger note will always be worth as many *tactus* as the number of semibreves it contains, unless proportions, augmentation or diminution alter this, as we will show next.

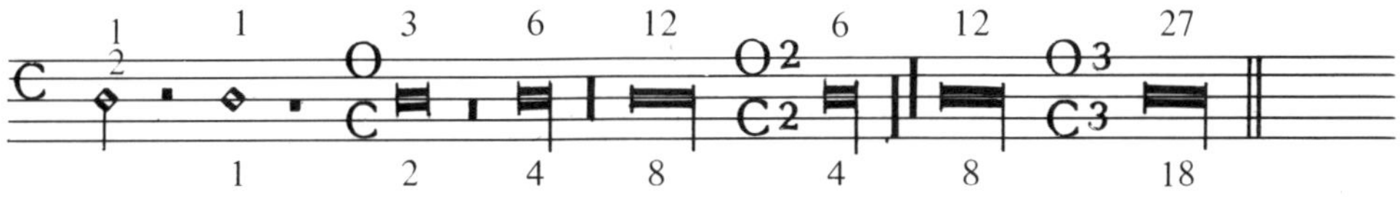

CHAPTER 5

Proportions

In teaching proportions I follow here the commonly accepted practice of discussing them in a separate section. Yet their nature requires that they be reconsidered in the chapter on augmentation and diminution, since they are really nothing but a certain definite kind of augmentation and diminution, for they either increase or lessen the essential value of notes. So we who propose to discuss a definite, established practice of singing and not any subtleties of speculative mathematicians, wish to speak about them in a truly practical way.

What is the measurement of proportions?

It is a measurement in which two different numbers are compared to notes or to notes and *tactus*. For a proportion is established by comparison of two things. If they are equal in all respects it is called a proportion of equality, and if unequal, a proportion of inequality.

Here we speak of a proportion of equality whenever the number of semibreves and *tactus* are the same, just as we see them in church songs called *chorales*. But we consider them a proportion of inequality when the number of notes and the number of *tactus* differ, as when we sing two, three, four or more semibreves to one *tactus*, or when we give two, three, four or more *tactus* to each semibreve.

How many kinds of proportions of inequality are there?

Two, called proportions of greater or lesser inequality by mathematicians. But because of their effect we prefer to call them augmenting and diminishing proportions, for the former always increases the value of notes and the latter always decreases their value.

By what signs are proportions recognized?

By two numbers written one above the other. The upper number counts the semibreves in *dupla*, *tripla*, *quadrupla* and similar proportions, and the lower number shows the *tactus*. But in *sesquialtera* both numbers indicate notes and neither shows the *tactus*.

Which are the proportions of lesser inequality or diminution?

They are proportions in which the upper number is larger than the lower, as *dupla*, $\frac{2}{1}$, *tripla*, $\frac{3}{1}$, *quadrupla*, $\frac{4}{1}$, *sesquialtera*, $\frac{3}{2}$, *sesquitertia*, $\frac{4}{3}$, and others of this genus. We still want to call them diminishing proportions here, because they always equate more semibreves with fewer *tactus*, since they truly lessen the value of these notes. Thus it will be necessary for each of them to be sung with a value somewhat less than a complete *tactus*.

But in order to allow young boys to understand this subject correctly I will describe in particular those proportions of this genus which are more commonly used, and I will add an example of each. The fact that many other proportions are considered by mathematicians means nothing to me here, since I have planned to treat only those proportions which the more general practice of singing demands.

Proportio dupla

What is *proportio dupla*?

It is a proportion which lessens by one half the value of notes and rests of every kind, so that in it two notes of the same kind are worth no more than one was formerly worth. This is why we call it a diminishing proportion, since it makes a breve from a long, a semibreve from a breve, and a minim from a semibreve. It is called *dupla* with regard to a complete semibreve, for it makes two semibreves equal to one.

How is it written?

It has two numbers written one above the other, the upper of which contains the lower twice with nothing remaining, as one can see in these numbers: $\frac{2}{1}$, $\frac{4}{2}$, $\frac{6}{3}$, $\frac{12}{6}$. But young students should know that whenever a line intersects the middle of a circle, as ⦶, ₵, or number two follows a circle, as O2, C2, or a half circle is reversed, as Ɔ, *proportio dupla* is always meant.

Example of *proportio dupla*.
Ex. 21 [*Benedictus* from *Missa Gaudeamus* — Josquin des Prez]

But why are the proportional numbers written a little later in inverted order?

When this happens in proportions it means that the proportion ceases at this point, and that the notes which follow are to be considered again according to the sign which just preceded the proportion, unless a different sign or a different proportion follows. In that case it is not necessary to invert the numbers to cancel the proportion, since it is necessary to yield to the following signs and not to return to the preceding signs. This will be seen very clearly in the seventh chapter on resolutions.

Proportio tripla

What is *proportio tripla*?

It is a proportion in which a perfect breve or three semibreves fit a *tactus* of one complete semibreve. In this way a semibreve retains only one third of its essential value. We emphasize the perfect breve here because everything that has been stated earlier about the perfection and imperfection of *tempus* and about the dot of alteration and division has a place also in this proportion and must be observed without exception, just as the proportion must always be measured in ternary groups.

How is *proportio tripla* written?

It has two numbers written one above the other, in which the upper number contains the lower three times, as $\frac{3}{1}$, $\frac{6}{2}$, $\frac{9}{3}$, etc.

Example of *proportio tripla*.

Ex. 22 [*cito anticipent* from *Dominum non secundum* — Marbriano de Orto]

What is *proportio quadrupla*?

It is a proportion in which four semibreves are sung to one *tactus*, that is, in which these notes retain only one fourth of their essential value.

How is *proportio quadrupla* written?

It has two numbers written one above the other, in which the upper number contains the lower four times, as $\frac{4}{1}$, $\frac{8}{2}$, $\frac{12}{3}$, etc.

Ex. 23 [*Ave verum, pars II* — Josquin des Prez]

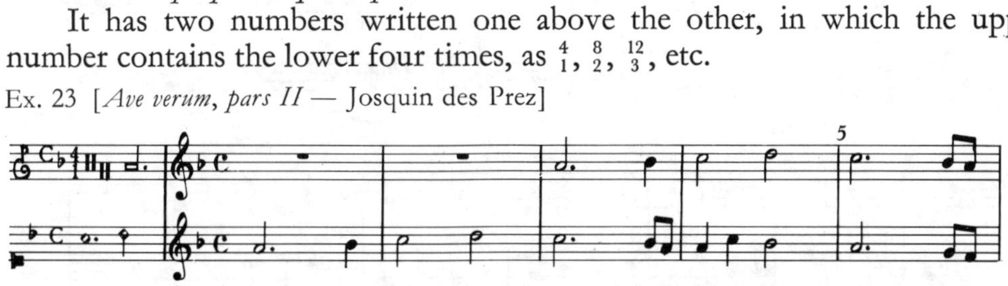

Proportio sesquialtera

What is *proportio sesquialtera*?

It is a proportion in which three minims or a semibreve and a minim are sung to one *tactus*.

How is this proportion written?

It also has two numbers written one above the other, in which the upper number contains the lower one and one-half times, as $\frac{3}{2}$, $\frac{6}{4}$, $\frac{9}{6}$, $\frac{12}{8}$, etc.

Ex. 24 Josquin: [*Fuga duorum. Agnus Dei II* from *Missa Malheur me bat*]

Proportio hemiolia

What is *proportio hemiolia*?

It is exactly the same as *sesquialtera*, for it is called ἡμιόλιος by the Greeks. I do not see any good reason why musicians want to distinguish one from the other, unless it is because blackening of notes alone, without other proportional signs, indicates that three semibreves in *tempus* and three minims in *prolatio* are given to each *tactus*.

Ex. 25 [*cum sancto* from the *Gloria* of *Missa Narayge* — Jean Ghiselin]

Now follows another *hemiolia prolationis*, but *diminuta*, to which the *discantus*, also *diminutus*, harmonizes through *proportio dupla*. The composer is unknown.

Ex. 26 [*Quem in sacrae mensa coenae*]

1 Heyden has c.

What is *proportio sesquitertia*?[32]

It is a proportion in which four notes of the same kind are sung in place of three, so that each of the notes loses one-fourth of its value. This is easy to do in maximas, longs, and breves, but it is harder in semibreves, and most difficult of all in minims, semimims and *fusae*.

By what signs is *sesquitertia* recognized?

By two numbers, of which the upper contains the lower once and one-third more, as $\frac{4}{3}$, $\frac{8}{6}$, $\frac{12}{9}$, $\frac{16}{12}$.

[32] The text and musical example of *sesquitertia* are lacking in the 1537 edition.

Ex. 27 Example of *sesquitertia*.

These are the proportions of diminution that are generally used in ordinary songs of the most excellent musicians. We believe that there is greater value in studying them more thoroughly than the remaining proportions. On this account it seemed proper to omit other proportions here, since they relate not so much to the practice of singing as to mathematical acumen. It is much easier to show the ratio of numbers in proportions of *multiplex superparticulare* and *multiplex superpartiens* than it is to perform their note values in singing, and I would readily believe that those who compose such examples can hardly sing themselves what they want others to teach.

What are proportions of greater inequality?

They are proportions in which the two numbers are written so that the upper number is always smaller than the lower, as in *subdupla* or $\frac{1}{2}$, *subtripla* or $\frac{1}{3}$, or *subquadrupla* or $\frac{1}{4}$, and so forth. In proportions written in this way one rule applies: notes and rests must be multiplied as many times as the lower number contains the upper. Thus *subdupla* doubles all notes and rests, *subtripla* triples them, *subquadrupla* quadruples them, etc. Since the matter is easy to understand, words are less necessary than examples, which will be found below in augmentation.

The preceding is all that need be taught about each proportion of augmentation and diminution that current practice of singing requires. Young students should study the material that much more diligently, since by far the greatest part of augmentation and diminution is indicated in this way.

CHAPTER 6

Augmentation and diminution

It frequently happens in approved songs that the essential value of notes and rests is increased or lessened by placing one kind of sign against another. The essential value of notes means that each semibreve equals one *tactus* under the signs O, C. Thus, if we give two, three, or four *tactus* to each semibreve we call it augmentation; if we give two, three, four or more semibreves to each *tactus*, we call it diminution.

There are two rules in particular through which everything that thus far has not been understood by many about various signs is now explained very successfully.

First rule: In every kind of song based on true art only one very simple kind of *tactus* is to be used.

Second rule: Every sign of augmentation or diminution in a song or proportion should be related to the essential value of a semibreve, the foundation, as it were, of every proportional sign.

Augmentation

What is augmentation?

It is the increase in the value of notes beyond their common and essential value by means of certain signs or canonic inscriptions. It is usually indicated in three ways.

First: by putting *prolatio maior* in one voice in opposition to *prolatio minor* in other voices, as ⊙, *O*, *C*. Through the inscribed dot a perfect semibreve equals three *tactus*, an imperfect semibreve equals two, and a minim equals one. Examples will be shown later in [chapter seven on] resolutions.

Second: by proportions of lesser inequality which we call augmenting proportions, that is, in which the upper number is smaller than the lower, as *subdupla* or $\frac{1}{2}$, *subtripla* or $\frac{1}{3}$, *subquadrupla* or $\frac{1}{4}$, and others of this genus. In such proportions all notes and rests are multiplied as many times as the lower number contains the upper.

Third: by canonic inscriptions, which indicate an increase of two, three, four, or more times. An example:

Qui tollis [from *Gloria* of *Missa*] *Ie ne demande* — Obertus.

From the following outline young boys can quickly learn everything that pertains to signs and proportions in augmentation. In fact, they may use this outline as a very definite rule in resolving augmented note values, as we will teach later in chapter 7.

Augmentatio inscripta per	⊙3 Ͼ3 ⊙ Ͼ	Triplicat omnes Perfectas Notulas ac Pausas, Imperfectas duplicat, alteratas quadruplicat.	
	$\frac{1}{2}$	Duplicat	Omnes Notulas ac Pausas, nullis exceptis
	$\frac{1}{3}$	Triplicat	
	$\frac{1}{4}$	Quadruplicat	
	$\frac{1}{5}$	Quintuplicat	

In the following chapter young students will find many examples of all these signs, together with their resolutions.

Diminution

What is diminution?

It is the lessening of the essential value of notes and rests by means of certain signs and canonic inscriptions.

How is diminution shown?

In four ways. First, by a number two written beside a circle or semicircle, as O2, C2. But I prefer the number written somewhat below, so that the number will show *proportio dupla* and not *modus minor*. Also in *proportio tripla* we will write the three obliquely below the sign and not beside it. In this way we know that *proportio tripla* and not *modus maior* is meant.

In the second way *diminutio* is shown by a vertical line drawn through the center of a circle or semicircle, as ɸ, ₵, Φ, ₵.

In the third way *diminutio* is shown by a reverse semicircle as Ɔ. In each of these three ways every note loses half the value it originally had, so that a semibreve is equal to only half a *tactus*, an imperfect breve equals a complete *tactus*, and a long equals two *tactus*. The following examples show this.

Example of the the first way, through C and C2 — *Duo in unum.*
Ex. 28 [*In nomine* from *Benedictus* of *Missa L'homme armé super voces musicales* — Josquin des Prez]

Example of the second way, through C and ₵ — *Duo in unum.*
Ex. 29 [*Qui venit* from *Benedictus* of *Missa L'homme armé super voces musicales* — Josquin des Prez]

Example of the third way, through C and Ɔ — *Duo in unum.*
Ex. 30 [*Benedictus* from *Missa L'homme armé super voces musicales* — Josquin des Prez]

In the fourth way *diminutio* is shown by proportions of every genus, as in proportions of greater inequality, in which the upper number is larger than the lower; earlier we decided to call them diminutions because they lessen the essential value of notes. They are *dupla* or $\frac{2}{1}$, *tripla* or $\frac{3}{1}$, *quadrupla* or $\frac{4}{1}$, *sesquialtera* or $\frac{3}{2}$, and so forth. Examples of them from chapter five should be reviewed here.

Diminutio per
ɸ3
¢3
ʘ2
Є2
O2
C2
ɸ
¢
Ɔ
$\frac{2}{1}$ } Dimidia
O3
C3
$\frac{3}{1}$ } Tertia
$\frac{4}{1}$ Quarta

} Parte omnes Notulas ac Pausas valere facit, eius valoris, quem alias absque Diminutione habebant.

Double diminution

Diminution of diminution occurs when an already diminished value is diminished again, so that only a half of one-half remains, as in ɸ2, ¢2, Ɔ̸, Ɔ. In these signs, which show double diminution by a vertical line and number two, or by a reversed sign and a vertical line, four semibreves are sung to each *tactus*.

But it is necessary here to bear in mind the proportional diminutions which are written under the signs of simple diminution, as ɸ, ¢, O2, C2, Ɔ, since in the previous signs *dupla* equated four semibreves with one *tactus*, *tripla* six semibreves with one *tactus*, *quadrupla* eight semibreves with one *tactus*, and *sesquialtera* three semibreves with one *tactus*. Unless this is the case I certainly do not see the difference between the proportional signs C3 and ¢3. It is surely necessary to indicate whether they are *integer* or diminished, unless perhaps one says that with the signs ɸ3 and ¢3 *proportio sesquialtera* is meant, and not *tripla*, so that three semibreves in diminution would equal two semibreves also in diminution.

Diminutionis Diminutio.
ɸ2
¢2
ɸ2
¢2
Ɔ̸
Ɔ̸
$\frac{4}{1}$
} Omnes Notulas ac Pausas tantum quarta parte eius valoris, quem extra Diminutiones alioqui habuissent, valere facit.

Example of various diminutions.
Ex. 31 [*Benedictus* from *Missa ad fugam* — Josquin des Prez]

1 Heyden has *c*

But[33] it should also be noted here that a good number of examples are found in which signs in diminution follow other signs that are also in diminution but which are very often dissimilar in shape, yet the diminution which follows also loses value because of the prior diminution, that is, it makes a double diminution, and thus *quadrupla* is formed from *dupla*, *octupla* from *quadrupla*, etc.

Example from *Prosa de Maria Magdelena* — Henricus Isaac.
Ex. 32 [*Qualis sit* from *Prosa*: *Coeli terrae maris*]

Syncopation

What is syncopation?

Syncopation is generally considered to occur whenever the mensural values of semibreves are sung for some time in opposition to the uniform movement of the *tactus*. Our brief advice here concerning this disparity is as follows: while singing do not allow the note values to return to agreement with the *tactus*, but persist vigorously in the disparity until the notes are reconciled to the *tactus*, for such a disparity hardly ever extends beyond the second or third *tempus*.

[33] Text and following example are lacking in the 1537 edition.

Ex. 33 Example [lacking alto and bass, from the *Gloria* of *Missa*] *Ie ne demande* — Obertus.

CHAPTER 7

Concerning a single, uniform tactus used in every different kind of song, and concerning the mutual resolution of various signs.

Everything that has been taught so far about proportions, augmentation and diminution should be mastered very diligently by young students, because there are very definite rules, like the surest threads of Medea, which they can follow as leaders and expeditiously traverse the labyrinths of changing mensuration signs. In order to establish their validity with certainty I will now present some very difficult examples of songs and will add their *resolutiones*, so that anyone can see what should be sung in them as in a mirror. But first let me say that I will give definite proof in songs of the best composers, songs which, since they cannot be sung by anyone who tries to use different kinds of *tactus*, will fully demonstrate through this that all signs, however diverse, in conformity with the art can and must be fitted to the measurement of the same *tactus*.

Ex. 34 First proof that different signs of *integra*, *diminuta* and *proportionata* can be sung easily and correctly to a single *tactus*. N.P.

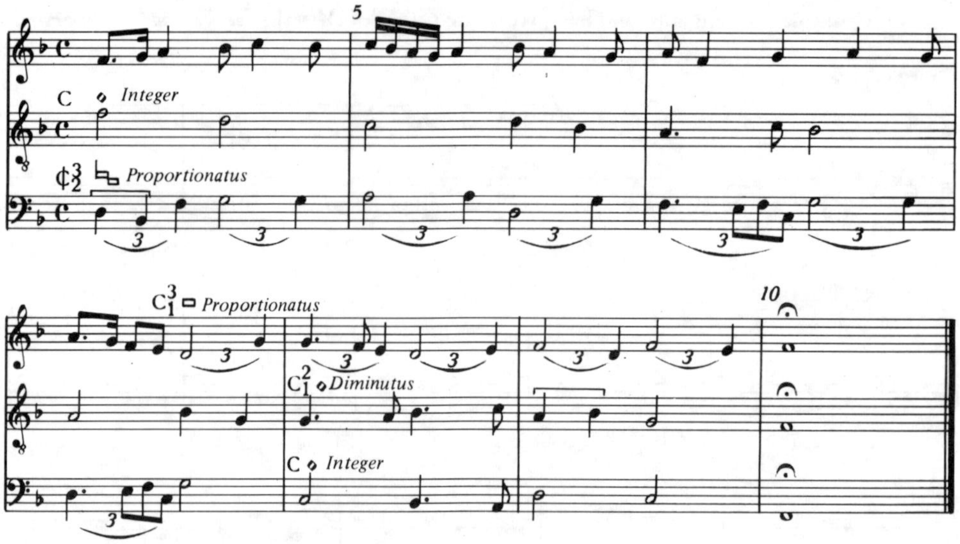

Second proof that signs of *integra*, *diminuta* and *proportionata* are sung to the same *tactus*. *Fuga trium* from *L'homme armé* by Josquin.
Ex. 35 [*Agnus Dei II* from *Missa L'homme armé super voces musicales.*]

Third proof confirming the same rule, by Petrus de la Rue. *Fuga* of four voices proceeding from one, in which the *discantus* is sung *diminutus*, the *tenor proportionatus*, the *altus integer perfectus*, and the *bassus integer imperfectus*.

Ex. 36 [*Agnus Dei III* from *Missa L'homme armé* — Pierre de la Rue]

Fourth proof of the same rule, by Henricus Isaac, is from the *Prosa de Conceptione Mariae*, in which *proportio tripla* is indiscriminately opposed to *diminutus* and *integer* note values.

Ex. 37 [*Prosa*: *De radice Jesse*]

What is a *resolutio*?

A *resolutio* is the transcription of more abstruse note values into a more common form. In order to do this correctly it is necessary to apply everything that was taught earlier about signs of *modus*, *tempus*, *prolatio*, *proportio*, as well as what concerns perfection, imperfection, alteration and division. For[34] the signs of *modus*, *tempus*, *prolatio*, etc., to be treated here are no different than those described earlier in successive order. The table of *resolutiones* given below will be easily understood by young students when they realize that it is nothing new, but is borrowed from preceding rules and is merely repeated here.

How many kinds of *resolutio* are there?

There are two kinds, for a song is resolved from larger signs into smaller or from smaller signs into larger. A *resolutio* from larger signs into smaller signs increases the values of notes and rests because larger signs are arranged according to smaller signs in *genus submultiplex*, that is, in augmentation. Contrariwise, a *resolutio* from smaller signs to larger signs lessens the values of notes and rests because smaller signs are arranged according to larger signs in *genus multiplex*, that is, in diminution. For all signs, however diverse, have a certain mutual proportion which must be observed in a *resolutio*.

These musical signs are nothing but indications of proportions, just as older musicians considered them, for they indicated proportions through certain

[34] From here to the first rule of resolution both text and musical diagrams are lacking in the 1537 edition.

characteristic signs rather then through numerical fractions. Perhaps they did this because characteristic signs define perfection and imperfection as well as proportion, which otherwise would have to be indicated by tediously repeating numerical proportions.

Therefore, when applying the rules given below by doubling, tripling, quadrupling or sextupling note values, young students should always remember to relate the notes and rests of a sign into which they resolve to what they resolve from by means of duple, triple, quadruple, sextuple, and similar proportions. On the contrary, when they see that the values of notes and rests should be lessened two, three, four or more times, they should refer the notes and rests of the sign into which they resolve to what they resolve from by *subdupla*, *subtripla*, *subquadrupla*, and similar proportions. As a result, the amount of value removed from notes and rests is always the same amount that is added to the numbers, and conversely, the amount added to the value of notes and rests is the same as that which is removed from the numbers.

Universal rule

Every augmentation or diminution of note values should be understood and reckoned according to the essential and complete *tactus* of a semibreve; in addition, all signs and all proportional numbers should be considered according to ○ and ☾, the undiminished circles of *tempus*.

How many musical signs are there?

There are three, for one increases essential note values, one lessens them, and one retains them. Their nature and difference is easily understood from the following table, in which it is also necessary to know that the rests which follow notes are equal to the notes and must be reckoned in the same way.

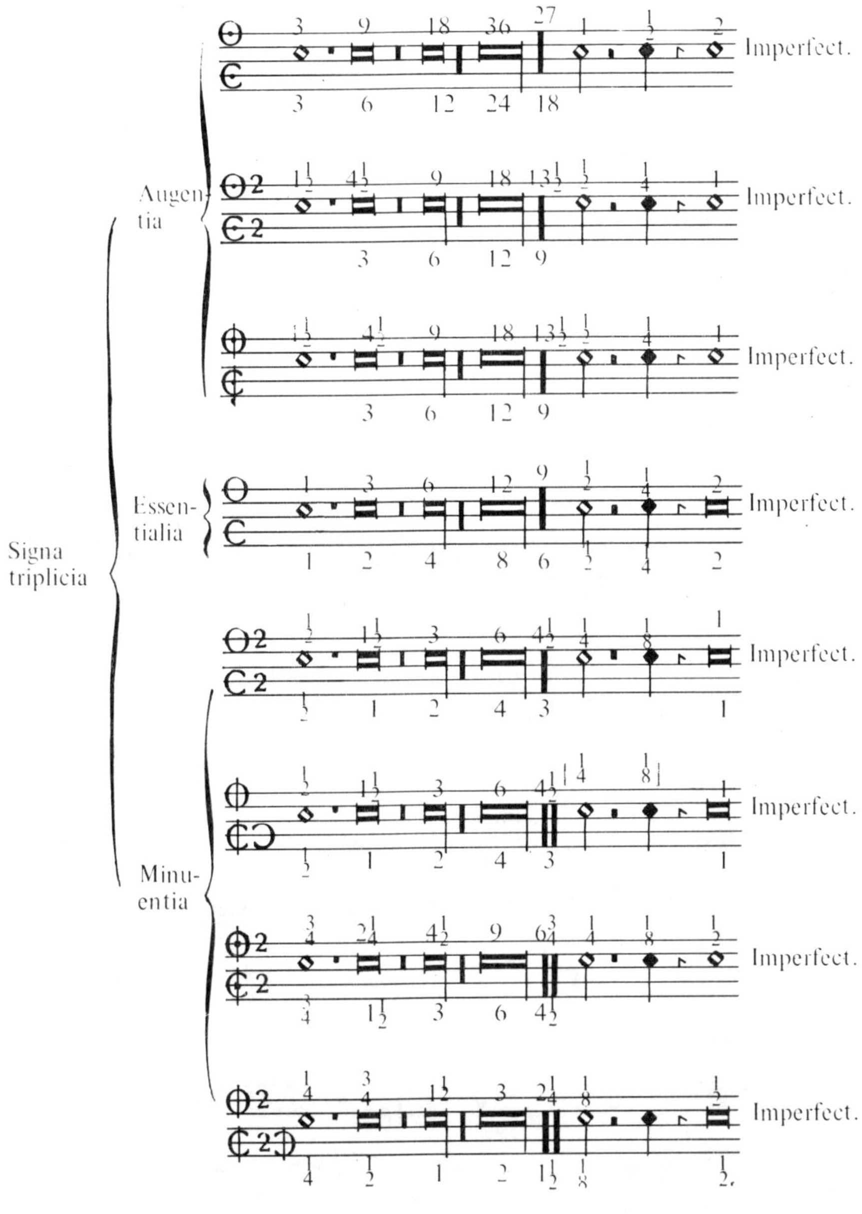

The[35] signs in this table are computed according to older music, so that perfect long rests show each *modus*, circles show *tempus*, and a number two always indicates *proportio dupla* and never *tempus*. The value of notes and rests in each *modus* can be ascertained from the enumeration of *prolatio* and *tempus* by merely observing which is perfect and which is imperfect.

The following are signs of *modi* according to more recent music.[36]

[35] This paragraph and the following example are lacking in the 1537 edition.
[36] In ⊙ 3 the breve should have 9 *tactus*, not 6.

Signa Modi Maioris recentiora.

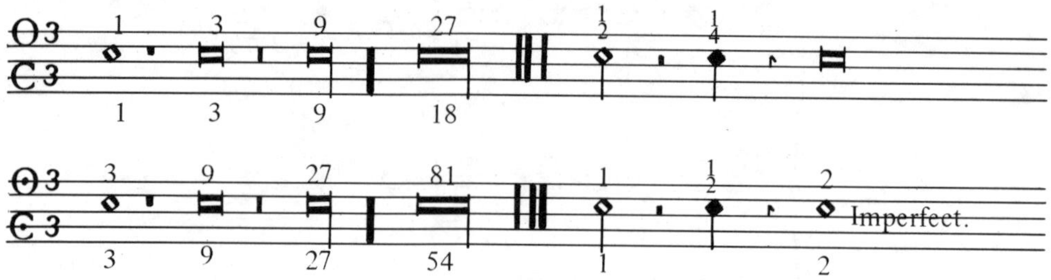

Signa Modi Minoris recentiora semper diminuta.

First rule of resolution from O, C, into ϕ , ¢, O2, C2, Ↄ.

When the essential value of notes is resolved into simple diminution, double the value of all notes and rests.

Example from *Naraige* by Ghiselinus.
Ex. 38 [Tenor and bass from Kyrie I of Missa Narayge]

Second rule of resolution from ϕ , ¢, O2, C2, Ↄ, into O, C.

When simple diminution is restored to the essential value of notes, remove half the value of all notes and rests.

Let the preceding *diminutae* voices demonstrate how half the value of their notes is removed with this example (39)[37] resulting:

[37] Ex. 39 has not been transcribed since it is the same in transcription as Ex. 38.

Tenor

Bassus

Third rule of resolution from ⦶ 2, ¢ 2, Ↄ̸, into O, C.

To resolve a doubly diminished *tempus* into *integer valor*, retain only a fourth of the value of all notes and rests.

Ex. 40

Fourth rule of resolution from ⦶2, ¢ 2, Ↄ̸, into ⦶ , ¢, Ↄ.

To resolve a doubly diminished *tempus* into a diminished *tempus*, remove half the value of all notes and rests.

Example [lacking alto and bass] from *Missa Fortuna* by Josquin.

Ex. 41 [*venturi saeculi. Amen.* from *Credo* of *Missa Fortuna Desperata*]

Fifth rule of resolution from C·, ⊙, into ○, C.

To resolve *integra* augmentation of *prolatio* into the essential value of *tempus*, triple all perfect semibreves and their rests, double imperfect semibreves, quadruple altered notes, or if they are already altered, double them.

A short annotation concerning perfect semibreves: here and in the following rules of prolation we understand as perfect semibreve notes and rests not only these simple forms, ◇ ▪, but also any others that are counted in larger notes and rests, as in breves and longs. But we consider blackened semibreves as imperfect, namely, those placed outside *hemiolia*.

Ex. 42 Example [lacking discantus and altus] from *Kyrie I* of [*Missa*] *L'homme armé* [*super voces musicales*] by Josquin.

Sixth rule of resolution from ⊙ , C·, into ϕ , ₵, O2, C2.

To resolve *integra* augmentation of *prolatio* into simple diminution of *tempus*, sextuple all perfect semibreve notes and rests, quadruple imperfect ones, octuple altered notes, or if they are already altered, quadruple them.

Ex. 43 Example [lacking *discantus* and *altus*] from *Christe eleison* of [*Missa*] *L'homme armé* [*super voces musicales*] by Josquin.

Seventh rule of resolution from ϕ , ¢, into O, C.

To resolve *prolatio maior diminuta* into *tempus integrum*, increase all perfect semibreve notes and rests one and one-half times, double altered notes, do not change imperfect notes except perhaps to make black notes white.

Ex. 44 Example from *Osanna* of *Missa Prolationum* — Iohannis Ockeghem.

Also belonging to the above rule is the example from this Mass that was printed on p. 74, likewise the example to be found later in Tone 5.

Eighth rule of resolution from ϕ , Ͼ, into ϕ , ₵, O2, C2.

To resolve *prolatio perfecta diminuta* into simple diminution triple all perfect semibreve notes and rests, double imperfect notes, quadruple altered notes, or if they are already altered, double them.

Example [lacking *discantus* and *altus*] from *Naraige* — Iohannis Ghiselin.
Ex. 45 [*Sanctus* from *Missa Narayge*]

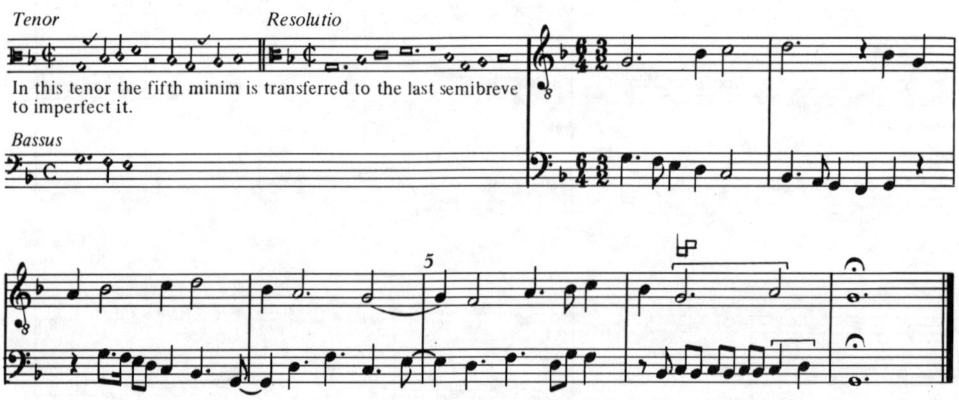

Ninth rule of resolution from ϕ 2, Ͼ 2, Ͽ, into ϕ, ₵.

To resolve *prolatio perfecta* twice *diminuta* into *tempus diminutum*, increase all rests and perfect notes one and one-half times, double altered notes, whiten black notes, and do not change imperfect notes.

Example [lacking *altus* and *bassus*] from Ghiselinus.
Ex. 46 [Latter part of *Sanctus* from *Missa La bella se siet*]

Tenth rule concerning proportional augmentation or *prolatio submultiplex.*

To resolve proportional augmentation or *proportio submultiplex* from *integer* into *integer* or *diminutus* into *diminutus*, always multiply all notes and rests as many times as the lower number contains the upper. An earlier example of augmentation is found on p. 92.

Eleventh rule: to resolve proportional augmentation or *proportio submultiplex* from *non diminutus* into *diminutus*, double whatever the lower number of the proportion indicates.

An example of *subtripla*, *subdupla*, and *dupla proportio* resolving into ϕ , ₵.

[Gloria from Missa Gratieusa — Ghiselin]

Twelfth rule: to resolve many different signs of a single melody into some other sign, relate each of them in turn to the one into which it resolves according to the prescribed rules.

Resolutio ex	⊙ ⦶̇ Ċ ₵̇ ⦶ ₵	in	O C	secundum	Quintum Septimum Quintum Septimum Secundum Secundum	Canonem

Example of Ghiselinus
[*Qui tollis* from *tenor* part in *Gloria* of *Missa Gratieusa.*]

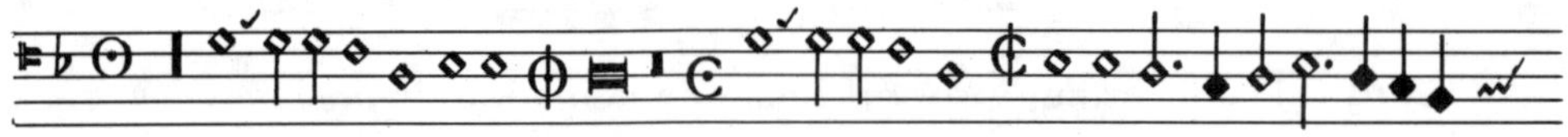

Qui tollis

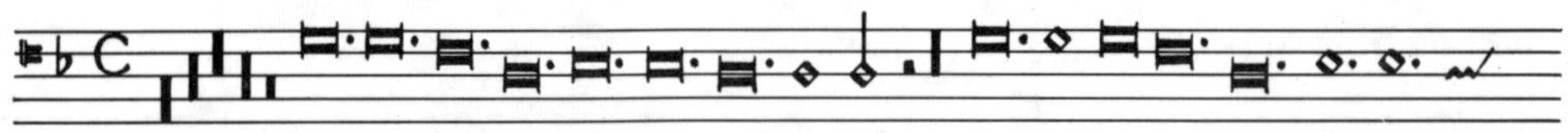

Resolutio in integrum.

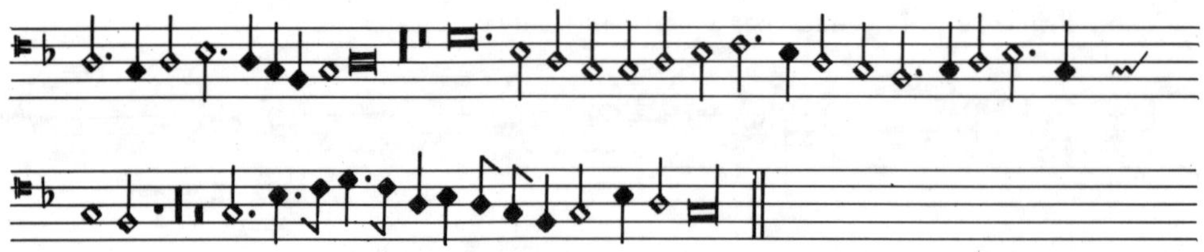

Resolutio eiusdem exempli ex		in		secundum		Canonem
	⊙		Φ		Sextum	
	Φ		¢		Octavum	
	C with dot (Ͼ)		O2		Sextum	
	¢		C2		Octavum	
	O				Primum	
	C				Primum	

Resolutio in Diminutum.

Another example of Ghiselinus.

Resolutio scilicet ex	Φ Φ2 ₵ ₵2 Φ2	in	Φ ₵	secundum	Octavum Nonum Octavum Nonum Quartum	Canonem.

The first and second minims at the beginning of this example belong to the first breve following them, so that it is worth eight minims.

[*Et resurrexit* from *tenor* part in *Credo* of *Missa Gratieusa*]

Resolutio præcedentis exempli.

In the following example the placement of both the number and the mensuration signs must be observed, because according to their position the notes should be transcribed and sung first in a rising and then a descending pattern.

Last *Agnus* from *La belle* by de Orto.[38]
[*Agnus Dei III* from *discantus* in *Missa La bella se sied* by Marbriano de Orto.]

These[39] are the things I wished to teach concerning musical signs, in so far as they are contained in established art and definite rules. For other things that are entirely lacking in art and rules, and there are indeed many, I consider to be meaningless to myself who have tried to prescribe rules and not enigmas or idle fancies.

But there are some things that can be corrected easily through art, such as if the value of C, a *non diminutus* semicircle, is doubled because it is used opposite ₵, a sign of diminution, or if diminution is applied to a *non diminutus* ⋶ in *prolatio perfecta*, or if *sesquialtera* is understood in *prolatio perfecta* when no numbers are present. In the first of these the error is small and due to ignorance of the art, since what is halved was taken for *integer*, and what is *integer* was doubled, while the art plainly indicates a proportion of one-half to *integer* and

[38] Petrucci (*Misse De Orto*, 1505) prints the canon: *Sequentibus signis*. In place of Heyden's two double bars he has two triple bars, which is more accurate, since each melodic segment occurs three times on different scale steps. In Petrucci's *resolutio* $\substack{O\\3}$ is used in place of Heyden's $\substack{3\\1}$.

[39] This paragraph and the following one are lacking in the 1537 edition.

integer to *dupla*. In the second case a bisecting line should be added to make ¢, and in the third case it is absolutely necessary to add numbers, as $\odot^{3}_{2}$. In other songs in which neither such a correction nor our rules can be applied, I grant every judgment made by their composers or by followers of the composers, and I will not oppose any liberty they take provided that they remember this one point: no art can exist which is not bound by its own clearly established rules.

No definite rule can be given about enigmatic canons which are frequently added to songs, except to observe the relative significance of the inscriptions, for they generally assume a subject's nature, usage, similitude or contrariety of meaning. Thus *cancrisare* means to move in retrograde motion. *Noctem in diem vertere* means to sing as white the notes that are written black, and *misericordia et veritas sibi obviasse*[40] means that a melody should be sung normally in one voice part while its retrograde version is sung in another.

CHAPTER 8

Tones

Here I will purposely refrain from describing Tones at length. For why is it necessary to pursue religiously the ranges of authentic and plagal Tones, as they are called, and the *differentiae* added to them, when we know that they have almost no meaning in figural music? So it is sufficient here to show as simply as possible how Tones of more commonly known *cantilenae* should be recognized, and how psalm tones and the *Magnificat*, as it is called, should be intoned. Anyone who wishes more details should seek it from other sources.

What is a Tone?

It is a certain definite quality of melody, or rather an affect of a song. For just as some affections of the mind are happy and pleasing, or grave and sedate, and others are sad and mournful, or angry and violent, so also the melodies of songs are distinguished variously in music because some differ in affect from others.

How many kinds of Tones are there?

There are eight Tones which are distinguished through certain intervals, each of which has a particular and special character. From the following verses young boys can learn very easily what these intervals are and which pertains to which Tone.

Intervals peculiar to each Tone: first, *re la*; second, *re fa*; third, *mi fa*; fourth, *mi la*; fifth, *fa fa*; sixth, *fa la*; seventh, *ut sol*; eighth, *ut fa*.

[40] A reference to Ludwig Senfl's *Crux fidelis*, which contains the canon: *Misericordia et veritas obviaverunt sibi*. In this motet the alto is the retrograde of the cantus, and the tenor the retrograde of the bass. An earlier source of the canon (and probably Senfl's source) is the opening composition in Petrucci's *Motetti A*, 1502.

Range of Tones: a higher range means an odd-numbered Tone, a lower range an even-numbered Tone. The number of a Tone is obtained from the end.

Syllables and final keys: first-second, *D*, *re*; third-fourth, *E*, *mi*; fifth-sixth, *F*, *fa*; seventh-eighth, *G*, *ut*; that is, the first and second end on *re* through *D la sol re*; the third and fourth on *mi* through *E la mi*; the fifth and sixth on *fa* through *F fa ut*; and the seventh and eighth on *ut* through *G sol re ut*.

What is a song of the first Tone?

Every song of the first Tone ends on *re* and forms its melodic line principally through the fifth *re la*.

Monodia Primi Toni.

What is a song of the second Tone?

A song belongs to the second Tone when the minor third formed of *fa* and the final *re* frequently occurs.

Monodia secundi Toni

What is a song of the third Tone?

It is a song which ends on *mi* and which chooses a greater part of its melody from the minor sixth *mi* to *fa*.

Monodia Tertii Toni.

What is a song of the fourth Tone?

One which ends on *mi* and which frequently repeats the perfect fourth with *la*.

Monodia Quarti Toni.

What is a song of the fifth Tone?

It is a song which ends on *fa* and which frequently repeats the *fa* a perfect fifth higher, or, as others prefer to say, a song which ends on *ut* and which frequently reiterates the perfect fifth *sol* and the major third *mi*.

Monodia Quinti Toni.

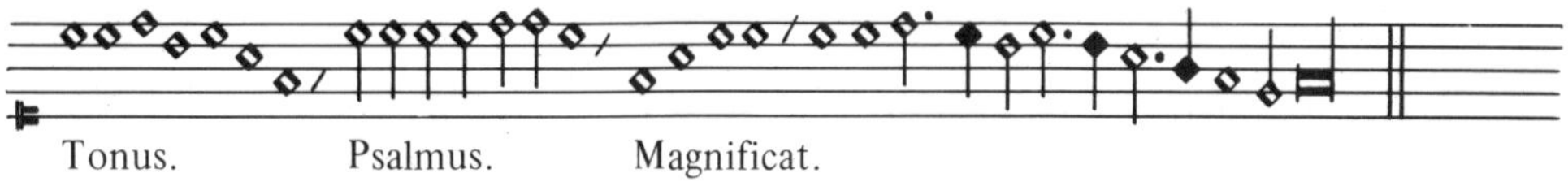

What is a song of the sixth Tone?
One which frequently repeats the final *fa*, with *la* a major third higher.

Monodia Sexti Toni.

What is a song of the seventh Tone?
It is one which frequently repeats *sol* and then descends to the final *ut*.

Monodia Septimi Toni.

What is a song of the eighth Tone?

It is one which forms its melody by frequent repetition of the fourth between *fa* and *ut*, the final.

Monodia Octavi Toni.

Example of the first Tone.

Ex. 47 *Pater meus agricola est* — Alexander Agric[ola]

Example of the second Tone.

Ex. 48 *Ave mater omnium* — Gaspar [van Weerbecke]

25
30
35

Fx. 49 Example of the third Tone.
Our previous remarks on p. 80 and also those in chapter six on various diminution should be reviewed in studying this bass. But the rules indicated below must be followed if one wishes to resolve the bass.

Example of the fourth Tone.
Ex. 50 *Agnus* [*Dei I* from *Missa*] *Malheur me bat* by Alex[ander] Agric[ola]

1 Heyden has a *semifusa*

Example of the fifth Tone — Iohannis Ockegem.
Ex. 51 [*Gloria* from *Missa Prolationum*]

20
25
30
35

1 Heyden's ligature reads *f, e, d.*

Example of the sixth Tone.
Ex. 52 *Agnus* [*Dei III* from *Missa*] *L'homme armé sexti toni* by Josquin.

10

Tenor proceeds in cancrizans

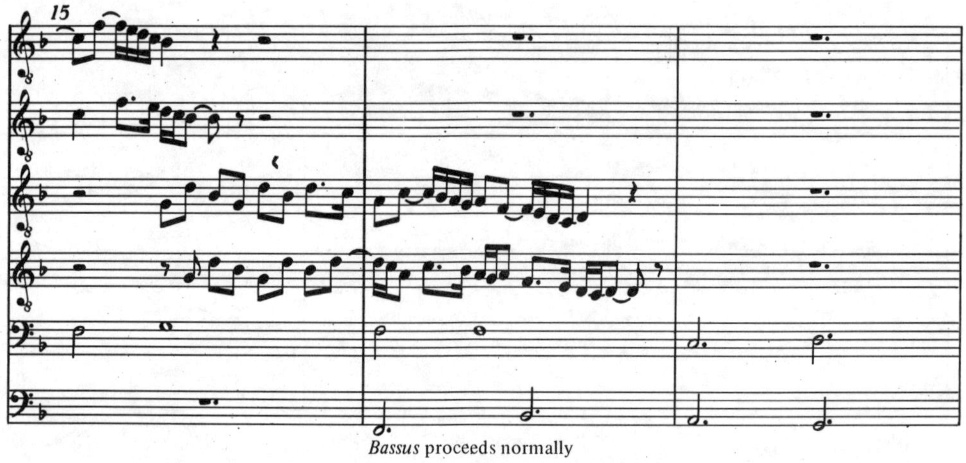
15
Bassus proceeds normally

20

Example of the seventh Tone.
Ex. 53 *Osanna* from [*Missa*] *L'homme armé* [*super voces musicales*] by Josquin.

1 Lacking in Heyden.

Example of the eighth Tone — Gaspar [van Weerbecke]

Ex. 54 [*Agnus Dei III* of *Missa Octavi toni*]

Iohannes Petreius in Nürnberg. 1540.

COMMENTARY

P.32, Ex. 1. According to Heyden's *tactus*-mensuration theory ₵ means that a complete *tactus* equals a breve. A suggested tempo is given in the Introduction. This is the first of nine compositions which Heyden did not identify, although he did not state that the piece was unknown to him, as he did in six other compositions. Josquin used the same music for the *In nomine* of the Benedictus.

P.40, Ex. 2. The composer is probably Nicolaus Piltz (Puls, Politus), of Nürnberg, whose lieder appeared in Forster's collections of 1540 and 1544. He was apparently a contemporary of Othmayr (b. 1515). See Hans Albrecht, *Caspar Othmayr* (Kassel, 1950), p. 51f.

It is possible that Piltz wrote this piece at Heyden's request, since it first appears in Heyden's 1540 edition and substitutes for a three-voice example by Rhau that Heyden had printed in the 1537 edition. In addition to being an example of solmization, it is the only piece in the treatise that has an unchanged *C* mensuration sign in all voices. It was reprinted in G. Faber, *Musices Practicae Erotematum*, Basel, 1553, p. 98.

P.42, Ex. 4. This piece is truly a puzzle canon. Heyden's directions for its resolution result in unsatisfactory counterpoint, especially in numerous open fourths. It could only work if there were an additional lower voice. Heyden's *resolutiones* are not always correct, as in Ex. 12.

The transcription of Ex. 4 produces satisfactory three-voice counterpoint. It can also be written a fifth lower; in that case the middle voice would carry no key signature.

P.43, Ex. 5. Smijers (*Missen XII*, p. 21) prints this Benedictus according to the Petrucci edition, which is a fifth lower than Heyden's and includes a *b* flat signature. Heyden transposed the music a fifth higher in order to provide an example in the discant range.

P.45, Ex. 7. This canon does not produce satisfactory musical results, which can be seen in the fourths in some measures, as m. 8 and m. 25. Possibly it is part of a piece with more voices, as the breve rest at the beginning seems to suggest. At any rate, the counterpoint in the canon is far from ideal. Heyden states that the composer is unknown.

P.47, Ex. 9. In view of the number of sources that contain this canon it must have been very popular in the Renaissance. In addition to Heyden, sources include Petrucci, Tschudi, Glarean, and Zacconi. Petrucci (*Motteti de passione*) and Tschudi (St. Gall *MS 463*) entitle it *Sic unda impellitur unda*; Heyden and Glarean do not give it a title, while Zacconi attributes the canon to Pierre Moulu and provides the text *Trinitas in unitate, unitas in Trinitate*. Both Glarean and Zacconi discuss the canon. For the latter's comments see his *Prattica di musica* (Venice, 1592), f. 45r; for Glarean's discussion see Clement A. Miller, *Heinrich Glarean, Dodecachordon* (American Institute of Musicology, 1965), II, 252.

P.52, Ex. 13. There are almost as many versions of this celebrated canon as there are writers who have resolved it. For a summary of a number of these solutions and also two by J. F. Levitan, see the latter's "Ockeghem's Clefless Compositions", *The Musical Quarterly XXIII* (1937), p. 440.

An opposing viewpoint to Levitan's solutions is expressed by Carl Dahlhaus, "Ockeghem's *Fuga trium vocum*", *Die Musikforschung* (1960), p. 307.

P.57, Ex. 14. The technical mastery of Senfl's *Fortuna* is remarkable. The tenor, carrying the *Fortuna* melody, sings it twice, m. 1-58 and m. 59-116. At the same time the discant goes up and down the *C* hexachord twice, each rise and fall corresponding to a complete *Fortuna* setting in the tenor. But most interesting is the fact that the discant consists of two exact mirror inversions of its melody. Thus in mirror inversion m. 1-22 = m. 29-57 and m. 58-75 = m. 79-116.

The symbolism in the music is unmistakable. The tenor represents the goddess Fortuna, and in the discant the two mirror inversions form two complete turns of her wheel. Her fickleness is shown by the vacillating tonalities, the discant having no signature and using the *C* hexachord, the alto and tenor having one flat in the signature, and the bass alternating between one and two flats.

P.72, Ex. 15. Exx. 15, 16, 18, 19, are discussed in my article in *Musica Disciplina* XXIV (1970).

P.75, Ex. 17. According to Heyden's theory ϕ means *tempus perfectum diminutum*, and this has been followed in the transcription. But the tempo is rather fast – it is likely that a tempo between O and its *diminutum* was intended by the composer.

P.80, Ex. 20. All sections of this Mass are based on hexachord patterns, which accounts for the lack of a signature in the discant and for the signature signs in the three lower voices. Heyden changed the mensuration signs in his discant and tenor from the original for didactic reasons. In Petrucci, *Misse Brumel*, 1503, all voices are in *O* and have no mensuration changes.

P.81. Concerning O3 as a sign of *modus maior perfectus*, Heyden says in *Musicae* of 1532: "this sign is rarely used because of its extreme slowness." His Ghiselin melodies and their resolutions are the same as those in the Petrucci Masses of Ghiselin, 1503, f. 24.

P.84, Ex. 21. See my article in *Musica Disciplina* XXIV (1970).

P.85, Ex. 22. Heyden substituted O^{3}_{1} for De Orto's ${}^{0}_{3}$ in Petrucci, *Motetti de passione*, 1503.

P.85, Ex. 23. This is another piece that Heyden does not identify, although he must have known it. The proportional signs are lacking in earlier sources, and seem to indicate that Heyden had difficulty in finding a suitable example of *proportio quadrupla*, so he simply invented one.

P.87, Ex. 25. Heyden again changed some mensuration signs. The signs in Petrucci, *op. cit.*, beginning with the discant, are: ${}^{0}_{3}$, ¢${}^{3}_{2}$, ¢, ¢. Tenor and bass move in blackened breves and semibreves.

P.88, Ex. 26. If Heyden wants the discant to be *diminutus*, as he says, then the other voices should have ¢*2* as a mensuration sign.

P.90, Ex. 27. The *tactus* indications at the beginning are made on the basis of ¢ as *integer valor*.

P.93, Exx. 28, 29, 30. These examples of *diminutio* show *proportio dupla* respectively through C2, ¢, Ↄ. See *Musica Disciplina* XXIV (1970).

P.95, Ex. 31. Most of the mensural complications of this Benedictus were created by Heyden. In Petrucci's *Missarum Josquin*, 1514, all voices begin with ¢, change to O^{3}_{2} in the middle, and return to ¢ near the end. Since Heyden's note values for C and O are half the value of Petrucci's for ¢, their tempo is the same.

P.96, Ex. 32. This prosa comes from the Mass *In festo Mariae Magdalensae* in Book II of *Choralis Constantinus*. Cf. *DTÖ XVI*, 111.

P.97, Ex. 34. Apparently Heyden wanted to give Piltz special recognition through his placement of Piltz's two compositions. The first, Ex. 2, is the first of the series of solmization examples, and Ex. 34 is the first of four "proofs" of the *tactus*-mensuration theory.

P.98, Ex. 35. See my article in *Musica Disciplina* XXIV (1970).

P.99, Ex. 36. The *resolutiones* of Ex. 36 follow those in Petrucci, *Missa Petri de la Rue*, 1503. Exx. 35, 36, and 37 demonstrate Heyden's theory so well in their original notation and mensuration signs, without any substitutions or changes on his part, that he probably considered them a kind of cornerstone of his principles.

P.104. In the four signs of "more recent" *modus maior* it is important to remember that O3 and C3 are based on a semibreve, while ⊙3 and Ͼ3 are based on a minim; also that the circle and semicircle refer to *modus*, not *tempus*. Thus in O3 all relationships are perfect except prolation; in C3, *modus maior* is also imperfect; in ⊙3 everything is perfect; and in Ͼ3, *modus maior* or the measurement of a maxima is imperfect.

The four signs of *modus minor* have a similar plan, but they are always *diminuta* and the circle or semicircle governs the measurement of a long.

P.105, Ex. 41. Since Heyden did not print the bass for this example the counterpoint is faulty, as the open fourths in m. 1 and m. 3.

P.107, Ex. 44. Just as in Ex. 16, Heyden considers the tenor and bass mensuration signs incorrect and copyists errors, since they lack the *diminutum* signs.

P.108, Ex. 45. In Petrucci's print of this tenor the *resolutio* agrees with Heyden, but the original mensuration sign in Petrucci's tenor is Ͼ.

P.108, Ex. 46. Heyden's tenor and its *resolutio* agree with Petrucci's print of 1503.

P.116, Ex. 47. Both Exx. 47 and 48 come from Petrucci's *Motetti Libro quarto*, 1505.

P.120, Ex. 49. In order to make the mensuration sign O2 a sign of *diminutum* Heyden changed the bass signs through special instructions for each sign, making each of them worth one-half of their normal value. The bass melody consists of an ostinato which repeats with rhythmic and melodic variations.

P.126, Ex. 52. Both tenor and bass carry the *L'homme armé* melody simultaneously. The tenor begins (m. 1-12) with the middle portion of the melody and then repeats it in cancrizans (m. 13-25). The bass has the first part of the tune in cancrizans (m. 1-15) and then in normal motion (m. 16-25).

P.129, Ex. 53. The *Osanna* presents an interesting problem of tempo. The tenor ⊙ would ordinarily mean augmentation according to Heyden, and in fact was given that resolution in other tenor sections of the Mass in Petrucci's *Misse Josquin*, 1502. But the canon *gaudet cum gaudentibus*, added to the *Osanna's* tenor, and the Ͼ3 in the other voices, which are the "rejoicers" of the canon, seem to indicate a quicker movement in note values. This interpretation of the canon is confirmed by Hermann Finck, although he also allows a slower movement. In *Practica musicae*, 1556, fol. CC, he says: "This canon is found when some sign, especially a sign of *prolatio maior*, is added to one voice part. The remaining voices are placed in *proportio tripla*, although they can be sung according to the requirement of either sign." For a study of the mensuration signs in this Mass see Charles E. Hamm, *A Chronology of the Works of Guillaume Dufay* (Princeton, 1964), p. 160ff.

BIBLIOGRAPHY

Agricola, Alexander, *Opera Omnia,* ed. E. Lerner. American Institute of Musicology (*CMM* 22), 1966.

Albrecht, Hans, *Caspar Othmayr*, Kassel, 1950.

Ambros, A., *Geschichte der Musik*, Leipzig, 1891.

Apel, Willi, *The Notation of Polyphonic Music*, Cambridge, 1953.

Auda, A., *Theorie et Pratique du Tactus*, Brussels, 1965.

Cicero, *Phillipics*.

Collins, Michael B., "The Performance of Sesquialtera and Hemiolia in the 16th Century", *Journal of the American Musicological Society, XVII* (1964).

Dahlhaus, Carl, "Ockeghem's *Fuga trium vocum*", *Die Musikforschung* (1960).

— "Zur Theorie des Tactus im 16. Jahrhundert", *Archiv für Musikwissenschaft* (1960).

Du Cange, C., *Glossarium Mediae et Infimae Latinitatis*, Paris, 1840-1850.

Faber, Gregory, *Musices practicae*, 1553.

Fano, F., "Heinrich Isaac Messe", *Archivium Metropolitanum Mediolanense*, 1964.

Finck, Hermann, *Practica Musicae*, 1556.

Geering, A., "Senfl", *Musik in Geschichte und Gegenwart, XII.*

Ghiselin, Johannes-Verbonnet, *Opera Omnia*, ed. C. Gottwald. American Institute of Musicology (*CMM* 23).

Hamm, C., *A Chronology of the Works of Guillaume Dufay*, Princeton, 1964.

Heyden, Sebald, *De Arte Canendi*, Nürnberg, 1540.

— *Musicae, id est artis canendi libri duo*, Nürnberg, 1537.

— *Musicae* Στοιχείωσις, Nürnberg, 1532.

Horace, *Satires*.

Isaac, Heinrich, *Van Ockeghem tot Sweelinck*, ed. A Smijers. Amsterdam, 1951, No. 52.

Isadore, St., "Etymologiarum", *Patrologia Latina, LXXXII.*

Kosel, A., *Sebald Heyden*, Wurzburg, 1940.

Krautwurst, Franz, "Heyden", *Die Musik in Geschichte und Gegenwart*, VI.

Levitan, J. F., "Ockeghem's Clefless Compositions", *The Musical Quarterly*, XXIII (1937).

Liber Usualis. Tournai, 1947.

Lowinsky, E., "Mattheus Greiter's *Fortuna*", *The Musical Quarterly, XLIII* (1957).

Mendel, Arthur, "Some Ambiguities of the Mensural System", *Studies in Music History: Essays for Oliver Strunk*, Princeton, 1968.

Miller, Clement A., "Erasmus on Music", *The Musical Quarterly, LII* (1966).

— *Franchinus Gaffurius, Practica Musicae*, American Institute of Musicology, 1968.

— *Heinrich Glarean, Dodecachordon, Ibid.*, 1965.
— *Johannes Cochlaeus, Tetrachordum Musices, Ibid.*, 1969.
Neue Deutsche Biographie, 1952-
Obrecht, Jacob, *Werken*, ed. J. Wolf.
Ovid., *Remedia Amores.*
Petreius, Johannes, *Liber Quindecim Missarum*, 1539.
Petrucci, Ottaviano, *Misse Alexandri Agricola*, 1504.
— (*Misse*) *Brumel*, 1503.
— *Misse De Orto*, 1505.
— (*Misse*) *Joannes Ghiselin*, 1503.
— *Misse Gaspar*, 1507.
— *Misse Henrici Izac*, 1506.
— *Misse Josquin*, 1502.
— *Misse Obrecht*, 1504.
— *Motetti A.*, 1508.
— *Motetti Libro Quarto*, 1505.
Plato, *Cratylus.*
Praetorius, Ernst, "Die Mensuraltheorie des Franchinus Gafurius", *Publikationen der Internationalen Musikgesellschaft*, Beiheft II, Leipzig, 1905.
Rhau, Georg, *Enchiridion Utriusque Musicae Practicae*, 1532.
Riemann, H., *History of Music Theory*, trans. R. Haggh, Lincoln, 1962.
Rubsamen, W., "The International 'Catholic' Repertoire of a Lutheran Church in Nürnberg", *Annales Musicologiques V* (1957).
Sachs, Curt, *Rhythm and Tempo*, New York, 1953.
Seay, Albert, "The *Proportionale Musices* of Johannes Tinctoris", *Journal of Music Theory I*, 1957.
Wagner, Rudolf, "Wilhelm Breitengraser und die Nürnberger Kirchen- und Schulmusik seiner Zeit", *Die Musikforschung* (1949).
Zacconi, Lodovico, *Prattica di Musica*, Venice, 1592.

INDEX